What
Every Manager
Should Know
About
Training

What Every Manager Should Know About Training

or

"I've got a training problem"... and Other Odd Ideas

Robert F. Mager

Lake Publishing Company
Belmont, California

BOOKS BY ROBERT F. MAGER

Preparing Instructional Objectives, *Revised Second Edition*

Measuring Instructional Results, *Second Edition*

Analyzing Performance Problems, *Second Edition*
  (with Peter Pipe)

Goal Analysis, *Second Edition*

Developing Attitude Toward Learning, *Second Edition*

Making Instruction Work

Troubleshooting the Troubleshooting Course

The How to Write a Book Book

ISBN 1-56103-345-6
Library of Congress Catalog Card Number: 91-078265
Printed in the United States of America

1.9 8 7 6 5 4 3 2 1

CONTENTS

0 What's In It for You   1

1 The Name of the Game   5

2 The Tools at Your Fingertips   17

3 How to Penetrate Word-Smoke   33

4 How to Solve Performance Problems   47

5 How the Magic Goes In   71

6 How to Deal with Trainers   95

7 How to Get Your Money's Worth   111

8 How to Do It Yourself   119

9 Handy Checklists   135

Useful Resources   147

On the Walls of Time   149

0

What's In It for You

Many managers have just about had it with what they think of as the "training scam." They're tired of having their people taken away from their jobs to attend "training," only to have them return without any more useful skills than when they left. They're tired of having to "do training" just because someone said that their people need to be "developed." They're tired of having to wait for long periods of time for training help. They're fed up with the let's-have-fun trainers who are more concerned with the quality of their own performance than with the performance of the trainees they are expected to serve. And they're angered when they discover they've been taken to the cleaners by trainers who sold them more training than they needed, or who took longer to develop it than was needed, or by vendors who loaded them down with training hardware they didn't need.

But many managers who feel dinged by the training game are victims by choice. They are people who wouldn't dream of entering a high-stakes poker game without at least knowing the rules and something about the strategies, but who blithely buy training without knowing the territory. Some are even proud of their naiveté. "Balderdash," you hear them say.

"I don't need to know *anything* about training except the phone number of the training department! If I need training I just tell 'em what I want. It's their job to provide it." Managers who believe this are easy pickings and can be sold a bill of training goods without knowing they've been had.

But, just as you can win at poker if you know the game—just as you can get a better shake at the used car lot if you know the rules—you can win at the training game if you know the territory. With just a little coaching you can avoid the training scams that can drain your budget in a wink, as well as the unskilled trainers who see every situation as a nail to be whacked by their training hammer. With just a few insights about the rules of the training game, and the turf on which it's played, you can tap into your training resources for services that will knock your socks off in terms of the good they can do for you.

That's the goal of this book: to show you how to be a wise consumer of training and performance services. It will show you how to decide where and when training will do you any good, and it will show you how to avoid expensive training when there are faster and cheaper ways to get you where you want to go. That's not everything, but it will increase your power to sharpen the performance of your people—at a cost you can afford. And that's a lot.

WHAT'S IN IT FOR YOU?

Plenty. If you use training services, and especially if you have to pay for them out of your own budget, this book will help you:

- Determine why the performance of your people isn't meeting your expectations—and know what to do about it

- Ensure that your workers possess the job-relevant skills they need

- Get training done in the least amount of time and at the least cost, whether the training is obtained internally or from vendors

- Avoid having your people away from their jobs any longer than is absolutely necessary

- Save 100 percent of proposed training development and implementation costs when analysis shows that a non-training solution will work better

- Protect your budget against those who would sell you more training hardware than you need

WHAT YOU NEED TO KNOW

There aren't many things you need to know to make good use of available performance and training tools, and if you are an experienced manager you can consider yourself at least halfway there. After all, as a manager you know that the mission of management is to help the organization accomplish its goals and objectives; you know that the best procedure is *first* to decide on the objectives to be accomplished, and *only then* to think about the combination of people, machinery, and processes that will accomplish those objectives. As a manager, you also know that it's better to do it right the first time rather than to pay to have it done over again.

Up-to-date trainers operate a lot like that. You might say that trainers now apply to their field the same good sense that managers apply to theirs: *first* trainers decide on the outcomes they need to accomplish, and *only then* do they decide how to get there. Planning before action. This is an important framework, but there's more. There are powerful tools that will often get you the performance you need faster and cheaper than training. That kind of performance power isn't something you learned about in the schools you attended. Nonetheless, it's clearly in your best interests to know something about how to get it and how to use it.

So, to make cost-effective use of these training and non-training tools, you need to know:

- What it takes to make the performance you want happen

- How to make sure you will get the training and other services you need

- How to decide when to train, and when to do something else

- How to deal with trainers

- How to get full value—how to make sure your people don't lose the skills they've learned

- How to do it yourself

That's a lot of power for the little investment you'll need to make to get it. But these items are critical to your being able to get the best possible performance from your own people—at a price you can afford to pay.

1

The Name
of the Game

If you don't know the name of this game, you can get suckered into emptying your pockets in a hurry. You can get lulled into believing that you're getting a useful service when in fact the service has little or nothing to do with your needs. And the name of *this* game isn't *training*.

But if it isn't training, what is it? Let me explain it like this.

If you work in a manufacturing organization, you will have at least one maintenance person who is responsible for keeping the machinery and the equipment running. When a piece of machinery stops working the way it should, the maintenance people are called in to troubleshoot the problem—that is, to find the cause and to do the repairs. Although the maintenance function is important to the success of the organization, maintenance itself isn't the *purpose* of the organization. Although maintenance is necessary to *support* the purpose, whatever it may be, maintenance is something you do because you have to. That being the case, it pays to have one or more people around who are good at deciding when and what kind of maintenance is needed.

The same is true for other services. Just because you provide medical services for those who need care, it is not the *purpose* of your organization to plaster bandages all over people just because you have them. Medical services, like accounting and security services, are a means to an end, but not the end in itself.

Training is also a means to an end but not the end in itself. It is not the purpose of your organization to train people just because you happen to have a training staff. If you could hire people who are able and willing to do what was expected of them, you wouldn't need trainers. But it doesn't work like that, does it? Even if you have a staff of highly competent people, your world changes. The jobs change, the tasks change, the very mission of the organization may change. That means that somebody has to help others to develop new skills. It's as simple as this: If your organization has people on the payroll, someone has to make sure they have the skills they need. Somebody has to train them.

But only when the workers don't know how to do the tasks they need to be able to do.

Rule #1: *Training is appropriate only when two conditions are present:*

1. There is something that one or more people don't know how to do, and

2. They need to be able to do it.

Rule #2: *If they already know how, more training won't help.*

We don't train because the company down the street is doing it, or because it seems like the right thing to do, or because somebody thinks "employee development" always means training, or because the workers belong to a minority, or because we want to reward people by sending them to an exotic training location, or because somebody's idea of accreditation is based on hours in a classroom rather than on skill. We train only because there are things that people cannot do that they need to be able to do to perform their jobs. Training for any other reason is either a fraud or an extravagance—or both.

PERFORMANCE IS THE TARGET

If training is only a means to an end, what is the end toward which it strives? It's *performance*. To contribute toward the success of the organization, you need your people to perform their jobs. Unless they perform their jobs they cannot help accomplish your organization's goals and objectives. The products won't get made, the marketing won't get done, and new products won't get invented. If people don't do what they're supposed to do, regardless of how much they know, the organizational ship will founder. Therefore, the name of the game is to smooth the way toward an ability to *perform*, because it is through human performance that results are achieved.

The key word here is *do*. It doesn't matter that someone is highly knowledgeable or highly skilled. If that person doesn't *do* anything—if that person doesn't *perform*, in other words—the knowledge will be of no value whatsoever, and there will be no results, no accomplishments.

SKILL IS NOT ENOUGH

Training is indispensable when people need to know things they don't know at the time. However, performance requires more than skill.

Rule #3. *Skill alone is not enough to guarantee performance.*

The facilitation of performance is a joint effort. Just as surgeons alone cannot assure the health of their patients, and just as violins alone cannot create the sound of an orchestra, trainers alone cannot assure the job performance of the people they train.

Successful job performance requires the following four conditions—all of them:

- Skill
- Opportunity to perform
- Self-confidence
- Supportive environment

An explanation of these components will help you understand why you are a critical player in the performance game.

Skill

If people don't know *how* to do it, they *can't* do it. No amount of incentives or exhortations or threats will get them to do it. Without skill there can be no performance.

If they don't know what to do and how to do it, and if they need to be able to do it, then someone will need to teach them to do it. But skills are not developed merely by listening to someone talk about how to perform. Skills are developed and strengthened through practice, through the actual doing of those work tasks. This includes "mental doing" as much as physical doing. If trainees aren't required to practice thinking through the steps of a procedure, for example, the chance is slim that they will be able to apply that procedure when the need arises. If trainees aren't required to practice the tasks they are supposed to be learning—whether those tasks involve interviewing, selling, report writing, or repairing—it is unreasonable to expect them to be able to perform as needed. Skills are developed mainly through practice and through the immediate receipt of information (feedback) about the quality of the practice performance.

Self-confidence

When people don't *believe* they can do something, they may not even *try* to do it, regardless of the actual level of their skill. People don't voluntarily put themselves in situations in which they may be embarrassed or humiliated. Therefore, if they are given the skills they need but not the self-confidence in their ability to perform those skills, they will be unlikely to perform those skills on the job. It's just too risky for them. No confidence, no performance.

Self-confidence (the technical term is *self-efficacy*) is important because it influences performance in several ways. People need strong self-confidence if they are to be expected to continue their efforts to apply what they have learned and to learn new things. Belief in one's ability to perform makes a person less vulnerable to natural on-the-job conditions that aren't always supportive. Self-confidence helps people survive in the face of rejection. It helps them persevere.

Skills don't automatically provide self-confidence. You may recall instances in which people with a great deal of skill didn't *believe* they had the degree of skill they did. You've probably seen people hang back because of a lack of self-confidence rather than because of a lack of skill.

It would be a mistake to think that belief in an ability to perform a task is created merely through the addition of knowledge and skill or by some generic "confidence-building" exercise. Rather, self-confidence is built through the conditions and consequences that accompany the practice of the skills to be learned. If there is no practice, of course, there is little chance that a belief in the ability to perform those skills will develop. But practice is not enough. The practice must be designed to lead to positive consequences, such as a series of successes, or comments intended to praise the performance rather than to belittle it. The instructional environment must provide opportunities for the trainees to judge their own level of competence. Training must be orchestrated so that trainees learn to accredit their successes to their own performance, rather than to the influence of others or to chance.

This is a serious matter. When childhoods are filled with, "What makes you think you can do *that?*" and "You're nothing but a lazy bum" and "Is *that* the best you can do?" and "You'll never amount to anything" and "How come it's just an A-*minus?*" they are taught to believe not only that their skills are inadequate but that they themselves are unworthy. Entire lifetimes can be ruined by such treatment. And when trainees in a classroom are ridiculed by the instructor, or are demeaned in any way by their superiors when attempting to demonstrate their skill, their self-confidence is likely to be eroded. A belief in one's own ability to perform can be so shattered that a person will give up in the face of even the smallest failure. No self-confidence, no performance.

Opportunity to Perform

Without the opportunity to perform, there will be no performance. Opportunity means being provided with items such as:

- The permission (or authority) to perform
- Information about expectations

- Tools and equipment needed to perform
- A place in which to perform
- The time to perform

If you were an accomplished bassoonist but didn't have a bassoon, you wouldn't be able to perform bassoon solos. No bassoon, no performance. By the same token, if you had a bassoon but lived in a state where bassooning is prohibited, you wouldn't be able to perform (without running the risk of being caught by the antibassooning police). If you don't have the tools to do your job, or a place in which to do it, you won't be able to perform. No opportunity, no performance.

But there's more, because mere opportunity to perform is not enough.

Rule #4: *You can't store training!*

Or, as the trainers say, use it or lose it. Unlike fine wines, skills do not improve merely with the passage of time. Think about the courses you took in school. Are you as sharp on each of those subjects as you were when the course ended? No? Why not? You've forgotten a lot of the information or skills because you haven't used them—because you haven't practiced them.

You can think of training as an act analogous to filling a large tank that has a hole in the bottom. Unless you keep filling the tank, it will eventually run dry. Unless learned skills are exercised, those skills will deteriorate. *Use it or lose it.* That means that people need not only an opportunity to perform new skills but also the reason to exercise those skills—not six months or a year after they were learned but now. If they aren't going to use those skills for six months, it is wasteful to train them today. The shorter the gap between the learning and the application, the more likely it is that the skills will be there when needed. Insist, then, that training occur just before people have an opportunity to use the new skills.

I recall that, as part of a research project, I once had to test the performance of radar operators at various military installations. The performance of one young man I tested was so poor it was practically nonexistent, in spite of the fact that he had successfully completed the 32-week technician's course. When the colonel found out about the dismal test results, he bellowed, "Get that man in here!" When the young man appeared, the conversation, if you can call it that, went something like this:

Colonel: Didn't you get good grades at radar school, soldier?

Technician: Yes, sir. I did.

Colonel: Well, how long have you been here?

Technician: About six months, sir.

Colonel: (Ominously) Well? What have you been doing all that time?

Technician: Working in the motor pool, sir.

The poor technician hadn't even set foot inside a radar van for six months after leaving school, until just a day or two before our testing team arrived. Is there any question about why his performance suffered? There was no opportunity to perform. *Use it or lose it.*

Supportive Environment

Suppose that every time you sat down to work on a budget your boss came in and whacked you about the head and shoulders with a rolled newspaper or showered you with verbal abuse. How long would you continue to work on budgets? Or, suppose that you were ridiculed by your peers every time you offered a suggestion at a meeting? How long would you continue to offer suggestions? Or, suppose that every time you made a worthwhile suggestion you were required to head the committee organized to implement it? Or, suppose that every time you came in under budget, your budget was cut for next year? No supportive environment, no performance.

The fact is that people learn to avoid the things they are hit with. It doesn't matter how noble the cause or how important the task; if people find it punishing to do the things you want them to do, they will soon stop doing them. For example, if you want people to tell you what can be done to improve quality, you need to make sure they're not treated like messengers bearing bad news. If you want them to report dangerous practices, you need to make sure they aren't treated like lepers, or worse.

A supportive environment is one that encourages desired performance and discourages undesired performance. It is an environment in which workers are given reasons (incentives) to perform in the desired manner, a clear description of the results to be obtained and the standards to be met; it is an environment in which the workers' world gets a little brighter when they do it right, and a little dimmer when they don't. *When the consequences of performing well are upside-down—that is, punishment for doing it right and rewards for doing it wrong—desired performance will be difficult or impossible to sustain.* Examples of upside-down rewards and what to do about them will be described in Chapter 4.

Performance, then, requires the presence of skill, self-confidence, opportunity to perform, and a supportive environment. Take away any one of those ingredients and the performance will suffer or, worse, will never appear.

AN INESCAPABLE TRUTH

You may already have deduced the next rule.

Rule #5: *Trainers can guarantee skill, but they can't guarantee on-the-job performance.*

Your trainers can influence the skill and the self-confidence of your people. They can teach people the things they need to know and do, and they can strengthen their belief in the ability to do those things. They can guarantee that each and every trainee has developed the skills described by the objectives of the instruction. But they cannot guarantee that those trainees will actually perform on the job. Why not? Because trainers cannot control the opportunity to perform on the job and because they cannot provide the supportive environment needed for continued performance on the job.

Trainers do, however, have a responsibility to assist you in preparing for the return of trainees from a course. They also have a responsibility to help you decide how to make your work environment more supportive. But they can't take over your management responsibility.

Thus, although trainers can provide skills and self-confidence, only you can provide the opportunity to perform, and only you can provide an environment that encourages and supports performance at its best. And you couldn't change this situation even if you wanted to. You are a key player in the performance game whether you like it or not.

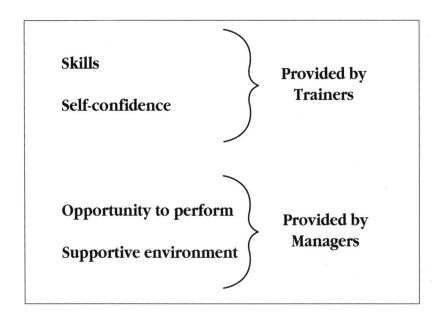

Rule #6: *Only managers, not trainers, can be held accountable for on-the-job performance.*

You can't just tell trainers to "train 'em" and then expect that the trained people will perform their jobs the way you want them performed. If the trainers taught what they were supposed to teach, and the trainees still don't perform as expected, it is not the fault of the trainers. You can't honestly blame the trainers for poor job performance, unless the trainees returned from the training without skill or the confidence to perform. (It's like horse-racing: If a well-trained horse is abused by the jockey, performance will suffer.) Although trainers can be held accountable for sending you people who have the agreed-upon skills when they return from training, they cannot be held accountable for poor job performance caused by lack of opportunity or support.

SUMMARY SO FAR

- Training is a means, not an end.

- Training is appropriate only when one or more person doesn't know how do something that he or she needs to be able to do.

- The purpose of training is to facilitate performance.

- Performance will occur only when the following are present: skill, self-confidence, opportunity to perform, and a supportive environment.

- Skills atrophy through disuse.

- Only managers, not trainers, can be held responsible for providing the opportunity to perform and the supportive environment needed for improved job performance.

WHERE WE'RE HEADED

Training isn't the only way to get the performances that will lead to valuable outcomes. There are other tools, almost all of them right at your fingertips. A look at what's in the performance "store" not only will make you a wiser consumer of training and performance services, it will show you tools that you can put to use immediately—often without help from anyone else.

2

The Tools at Your Fingertips

Suppose you go to your reputable auto repair shop because your automobile isn't working right. Based on what you know about cars, you imagine that you will need a complete engine overhaul and that the repairs will cost you hundreds of dollars. The mechanic, whom you trust, says, "Unless your heart is really set on an overhaul, I can solve your problem for less than 50 dollars."

Would you be interested?

Suppose you manage a large mill in which a major piece of machinery has shut itself down. Knowing that it costs your company 40 thousand dollars for every down hour, you imagine that the repair will be equally costly. But the troubleshooter, after locating the cause of the problem, says, "I can show you how to avoid this type of problem for less than a hundred dollars."

Would you be interested?

Or, suppose that because some new computer-controlled equipment is being installed in your department, you imagine that the operators will need a great deal of training. But after the trainers have reviewed the situation at your request, they announce, "Unless you have your heart set on a train-ing program, I think we can show you how to get your operators up to speed in less than a day."

Would you be interested?

These scenarios illustrate that often there are more ways to solve a problem than we are aware of—ways that are more appropriate than the one that first comes to mind. And, when the target is maximizing human performance, we can apply a number of tools. If you know what these tools are—if you know what cards are in the performance deck—you'll not only be able to make better use of training and performance services, but you'll be able to solve some of the problems yourself. Here's a list of the main tools through which to get performance results:

- Information
- Documentation
- Feedback
- Job aids (performance aids)
- Workplace design
- Organizational structure
- Permission (authority) to perform
- Consequence management (rewards and punishments)
- Training

Let's explore briefly each of these tools to see how it aids performance.

INFORMATION

One of the common reasons why people don't do what is expected of them is that they don't know what is expected of them. They may not know they have the authority to do something or they may not know for certain what they are supposed to do or they may not know the accomplishments they are expected to achieve. In other words, they don't know where the goalposts are or why they should get there. Trainers can tell you stories about workers whose performance instantly improved when at last they found out what it was they were expected to do. It isn't unusual to hear, "Oh, if I'd known that *that's* what they wanted, I could have done it" or "If I'd known they wanted it done to *that* standard, I could have done it."

Not only do workers often have to guess at what they are expected to do, there probably isn't one worker in a thousand who can clearly describe the results (or accomplishments) they are expected to achieve. Can you? Have you and your boss agreed on the outcomes (or accomplishments) you are expected to achieve?

Salespeople often can tell you what sales quotas have been established for them. But conversations with production workers often go like this:

You: What do you do?

Worker: I attach trundles to the forpals.

You: What results are you supposed to get? How will your success be measured?

Worker: Well, I attach the trundles to the forpals, the line moves on, and then I do it again to the next one.

You: If the person ahead of you on the line makes an error, are you supposed to fix it?

Worker: I don't think so. If I do fix it, it takes me a little longer to move the product along, and then they holler at me for holding up the line.

You: If something goes wrong at your own station, are you supposed to fix it or call someone else?

Worker: I'm not sure. But I don't think they'd like it if I shut down the line to fix something.

Although we always feel as if we've provided clear information about job expectations, we often send unclear messages. For example, suppose your boss told you to "be more aggressive" in doing your job. Would you know what you would be expected to do differently? Or, suppose you were told that you needed to make your department more efficient. Would you know what actions you would be expected to take—or what the outcomes of those actions should be? These may seem like rare examples. Yet, every day we use hundreds of words that don't carry the information we think they do. Here are but a few examples:

You should be a better team player.

You need to be more profit-oriented.

We need better flow of information.

Let's make this an efficient work organization.

We need better customer service.

You need to improve your cooperative leadership style.

Improve your poise and maturity.

Dress more sharply.

These words and phrases may describe something worth doing, but they don't give any information about what to do or how to recognize when success has been achieved. (You'll learn how to do that in Chapter 4.) Clear information about expected performance is a powerful tool for driving desired performance.

DOCUMENTATION

Another tool for promoting desired performance is documentation. It refers to information that is better stored somewhere other than in the performer's head. Documentation includes the manuals, the wiring diagrams, the schematics, and the reference materials that are supposed to make it possible for people to do their jobs. When these *exist,* are readily available, and are well prepared, they can make job performance a lot easier and smoother; when they are poorly constructed they can serve as a barrier.

Unfortunately, it is still common practice to write a user document as though it were an information repository—a bucket into which information is dumped. Want to get the information *out* of it? Forget it. Want to get the information out of it quickly? No way.

Because poorly designed documentation is a universal problem, you should always suspect that job-related documentation will provide you a rich opportunity for performance improvement. In other words, think of manuals and other documentation as getting in the way of good performance— that is, until proven otherwise. Why? Because company policy often insists that the documentation be written in stilted, nonfunctional prose rather than in language the intended user can easily understand.

Your trainers should be able either to provide you with usable documentation or to help you get it from other sources. Well-designed documentation provides an important steppingstone to performance.

FEEDBACK

Another powerful tool for improving performance is feedback. When people learn how well they are doing, or not doing, they have a reason to do better. When people don't get any feedback—information—regarding the quality of their performance, their performance won't improve. As you know, "feedback loops" are used extensively in manufacturing to ensure the steady operation of all kinds of machinery and processes. When a sensing device notes that a process is getting out of line, information is fed back into the system to correct the situation. Feedback is equally important in influencing the quality of people performance, and it is an important tool to those interested in maximizing job performance. Feedback is a powerful tool because it can lead to instant performance improvement and can help maintain high performance levels. It is almost always cheap and easy to implement.

It is a mistake to believe that workers automatically receive information about the quality of their performance just because they are doing their jobs; a job to be done doesn't always include information about the quality of the doing. For example, how often do receptionists find out how they affect the people they talk to on the phone? How often do you get feedback regarding *your* telephone peformance? For that matter, how often do you get specific feedback regarding the quality of *anything* you do? You see the point.

Some jobs require people to repeat a series of operations hundreds or even thousands of times each day—jobs designed in such a way that those doing them never once get feedback about the quality of their work. Consider the example of the production inspectors whose performance was called into question: "They read their meters with only 40-percent accuracy!" the manager exclaimed. He concluded, "They need training." But a ten-minute analysis revealed that although the inspectors were making hundreds (sometimes thousands) of readings each day, they never found out whether they were doing it accurately. They received no information (feedback) about the quality of their performance. When a simple feedback mechanism was installed, performance instantly jumped from 40-percent to over 90-percent accuracy. Cost? Negligible. Training investment required? None.

To be useful, feedback needs to be provided as soon after the performance as is possible. Delayed feedback has questionable value, which is why the annual or semiannual performance review should not be considered a source of useful feedback regarding the quality of job performance. It can't be. Although such reviews are important for other reasons, they are seldom helpful in correcting day-to-day weaknesses in job performance. Would your golf game improve if you got information about the correctness of your swing only once or twice a year? Hardly.

JOB AIDS

A key tool in the arsenal of those who would maximize desired performance is the job aid (also referred to as *performance aids* or *job performance aids*). Job aids are items that cue people to do their jobs right. They are used to remind people how to do things they already know how to do. You see them all around you and you use them all of the time. The lines painted on the factory floor help workers keep from stacking things in the traffic lanes. Instructions bolted to the gas pump remind you of the sequence of steps for pumping gas (which eliminates the need for an expensive national training program in gas pumping). The forms you are expected to fill out have boxes on them to guide your hand. You probably use some form of job aid to help you keep track of your appointments and to help you plan your day.

Checklists, road signs, telephone books, reminder lists, and other job aids are all around us. They help us accomplish tasks more easily, and they help eliminate the need for expensive training. (As a matter of fact, many training developers now consider the job aid the centerpiece of a training program. They take it as their task to design the job aids first and then to design training that will teach people to use the job aids. This can lead to a need for considerably less training than when job aids are absent.)

The importance of well-designed job aids should not be underestimated. I can recall reviewing an 18-week course, all of which could have been replaced with a well-tabbed binder of checklists. It would have taken no more than a day or two to teach people how to use the checklists (job aids), had they existed. Such examples are not rare.

To grease the way toward peak performance, see if one or more job aids won't make the work go more smoothly and more reliably. Your trainers can show you the list of conditions under which job aids are useful and can quickly create any you may need.

THE WORKPLACE

A well-designed workplace is another avenue through which performance can be facilitated. When the workplace has been designed properly, the work can be done smoothly. But when the workplace itself has been thoughtlessly put together, it can become an awesome obstacle to performance.

Once you think about it, you will realize that most work stations of the world were not designed, they were *assembled*. "Say, anybody using this chair? No? Okay, Farnswaddle, here's a chair you can sit on." "Anybody using this corner? No? Okay, let's put the new drill press there." "What? You need space for the new copier? I think there's room downstairs in the closet next to the restroom." And so it goes.

Workplaces that have been assembled rather than carefully designed almost always offer room for improvement. If you'd move that telephone from there to here, you'll save yourself a thousand steps a day. And if you'd allow people to have a coffee pot on this floor, you'd avoid their having to go seven floors down to the cafeteria for a break.

Performance professionals will always keep an eye open for opportunities to improve the workplace that has been assembled rather than designed.

ORGANIZATIONAL STRUCTURE

Sometimes it isn't the workplace that gets in the way of performance, it is the organization itself. Sometimes the organization is structured in such a way as to make it difficult for everyone to pull in the same direction. How many times have you been transferred from one person to another as you try desperately to get a simple question answered or to find the person who can be of help? How many times have you been impeded by "turf battles"?

When delays in getting things done are caused by the way in which organizational boundaries are drawn, it is appropriate to redefine the organization—to clarify goals, to specify the objectives that will accomplish those goals, to design jobs and interfaces between jobs that will smooth the flow of the processes through which outcomes are to be achieved.

The services of an organizational design specialist can be invaluable for reviewing the way in which work is currently organized and to suggest ways to make the work flow more smoothly.

PERMISSION TO PERFORM

It may seem odd, but it is not uncommon for people to be expected to do things they haven't been given permission to do. If people have been given the responsibility for getting results but not the permission to do the things needed to get those results, performing will be difficult, if not impossible. Lack of authority—permission to perform—usually is caused by simple oversight or by a misconception on the worker's part. Once identified, then, this barrier to performance is easily removed.

CONSEQUENCES
(REWARDS, PUNISHMENTS)

One of the most powerful tools for facilitating performance is at the same time the most available and the least well used. That tool is called consequences. These are the things that happen to the performers as a result of their performing.

Although favorable consequences for good performance are a sure way to get more of it, performing too often leads to punishment. That is, doing it the right way leads to hurt—to embarrassment, more scutwork, or some other form of punishment—because the supportive environment is somehow upside-down. It's easy to understand. If you were branded with nasty names, such as "whistleblower," every time you reported hazardous conditions, you would hesitate to do it again. As mentioned before, people learn to avoid the things they are hit with, regardless of whether they are being hit by force, by ridicule or humiliation, or by boredom or frustration. When a desired performance leads to that performer's world becoming somewhat dimmer, the act is less likely to be repeated.

The consequences of doing something right or wrong have a great deal to do with what people will do in the future. When performance is followed by events that the performers consider favorable, they are more likely to repeat the performance in the future. When their acts are followed by events that they consider unfavorable (punishing), they will be less likely to repeat those acts in the future. It doesn't matter whether *you* think an event is rewarding; if it isn't perceived that way by the person being "rewarded," it won't have the effect you want.

It should be no surprise, therefore, to learn that when trainers are faced with the "I need training" issue, they try to assure themselves that people aren't failing to perform because there is something topsy-turvy about the way the rewards and punishments are being dispensed. The consequence tool is not only at your fingertips; the fact is, you don't have any choice about whether you use consequences or not. Your only choice is whether you use them well or poorly.

TRAINING

It used to be that trainers...well, *trained.* If people didn't seem to have the right attitude, they were trained. If they didn't seem motivated or weren't performing their jobs, training was the magic bullet, the fix. It didn't seem to matter why people weren't performing well; the remedy was to train them. The rules of the training game were fairly simple. Want training? You got it. It wasn't so much that trainers didn't know any better; there just wasn't anything better to know.

This was not too surprising in an age when the training territory consisted mainly of classroom lectures and OJT (on-the-job-training). The lectures were usually offered by an old hand—a "subject matter expert" who knew little or nothing about training—who stood up in a classroom and hosed down a group of people with information. Little or no practice was given in the key skills to be learned, because telling was believed to be the same as teaching. Some instructors even prided themselves on their ability to walk into a classroom and "wing it"—that is, to instruct without preparation.

Because of the unsystematic way in which much training was selected, developed, and delivered, managers understandably learned to expect little in the way of results. They learned that it could take a long time to get the attention of the training department, that training would take people away from their jobs, and that when those people returned to their jobs, they may or may not be of any greater value than when they left. Training was just one of those things you had to send people to now and again. If people weren't worth more after the training than before, it merely confirmed the expectation that the training had no value.

But that has changed, and changed drastically. Even though some trainers are still allowed to practice like witch doctors in an age of modern medicine, trainers skilled in the craft now can actually guarantee that their training works— that is, that everything they do in the classroom will have demonstrable value on the job. Trainers know how to measure the important effects of training, and they know how to match the training to the needs of the individual trainee, doing so at least cost. And when training needs to be prepared practically overnight, the hotshot trainers even know how to do that. Skilled trainers can make training work so much better than in the past that sometimes their managers consider their tools to be "proprietary technology." Managers may even avoid publishing their results lest their competitors learn of this competitive edge.

A FLY IN THE OINTMENT

There's something about the application of the performance tools, however, that sometimes makes trainers uneasy. As already stated, training analysts know when a job aid—or other approach—will work better than training. They know how to analyze a situation and determine which approach will lead to performance improvement. But often they are reluctant to say anything to a manager whose operation would benefit from these non-training solutions. Why? Is it because they are afraid of losing "business" if they approached the problem with a different solution?

No. It is because managers sometimes notice shoddy performance and then ask for training. Managers may have already decided on the solution to the problem and may already have "sold" their bosses and peers on the merits of the plan. So they may not take kindly to a suggestion that there is a way to solve the problem that is faster and cheaper than training. They asked for training, and training is what they will have! Trainers, therefore, sometimes are hesitant about suggesting non-training solutions to performance problems. The result is that they feel pressured to develop a course they know is "bad medicine," because the person asking for it was unwilling to give up a poor decision to train.

By the time you have finished this book you will be able to guard against this expensive turn of events. If you keep in mind that your goal is to maximize the performance of your people, rather than to "train 'em," you will be able to make good use of trainers' services without spending an arm and a leg to do so.

THE PERFORMANCE TEAM

There are organizational units other than training departments that are directly concerned with the performance of people on the job. They are important members of the "total performance" team, whose services should be used when the need arises. Here are the main ones:

- *Human factors specialists* design work stations, as well as tools and equipment, that facilitate rather than obstruct efficient and effective performance of work.

- *Documentation specialists* strive to create documents—manuals, references, engineering drawings, and so on—that facilitate rather than hinder desired performance.

- *Health and safety groups* are charged with the responsibility for ensuring a healthy and safe workplace.

- *Organizational specialists* strive to remove obstacles to accomplishment caused by the way in which jobs and departments are designed and by the way in which they interact—or are prevented from interacting—with one another.

- *Methods and procedures specialists* strive to assure that the means by which work is accomplished do not themselves serve as unnecessary obstacles to accomplishment.

Each of these specialties can make sizable contributions to effective job performance, and it is worth seeking their input.

SUMMARY

The primary tools through which you can achieve maximum performance are these:

- Information
- Documentation
- Feedback
- Job aids (performance aids)
- The workplace
- Organizational structure
- Permission (authority) to perform
- Consequences (rewards, punishment)
- Training

You can appreciate why trainers often say "training is a last resort." Like surgery, training should be avoided when an easier and less expensive remedy is possible. But, also like surgery, when training is needed it needs to be done well, and it needs to be done right the first time. And that's a job for training professionals.

Now you might appreciate why so many trainers are moving to expand the name of their department to "Training and Performance Services Department" or "Performance Support Services." These full service departments are truly a source of performance improvement assistance and are becoming increasingly indispensable to the success of the organization.

WHERE WE'RE HEADED

To this point you've been made aware of the components required for effective job performance, and you've seen the main performance-influencing tools at your disposal. The next two chapters will teach you two key techniques. These are techniques that *all* managers need to be able to use, *whether or not* they have anything to do with trainers. Once you've mastered these techniques, you'll find yourself using them every day to get better performance from your own people, and from your trainers as well. But, should you make the mistake of thinking that these techniques are only for trainers to know about, you would be depriving yourself of two very useful management tools.

3

How to Penetrate Word Smoke

Imagine that you are an architect and a customer wants you to build a dream house. The conversation goes something like this:

Customer: I'd like you to build me a house.

Architect: Fine. What sort of house would you like?

Customer: Oh, a nice house.

Architect: What kind of nice house?

Customer: Oh, you know. Not too big, not too small. A cozy house.

Lots of words, but no help in telling you what kind of house the customer has in mind. Until you know something specific, it will be very difficult to know what kind of materials to buy and which construction crew to hire.

Let's turn the scenario around. Suppose *you* were in the market for a new house. Would you be willing to turn that architect loose with directions no more specific than nice and cozy?

Like it or not: the degree to which you speak in abstractions (fuzzies) is the degree to which you abdicate to someone else the power to say what you mean.

If you tell your trainers that you want them to make your workers safety-conscious, and you don't define the behavior you expect from your workers, the trainers will have to divine what you mean by *safety-conscious*. If you ask them to make your people customer-oriented, or to teach them to be empowered—without specifying what they would have to *do* to merit those labels—you abdicate to them the power to decide what you mean.

FUZZIES ABOUND

Thousands of words can be used in discussing human performance. Most words and phrases are abstractions—fuzzies—that are open to many interpretations. They mean different things to different people. Here are some examples:

- Conducts oneself in a professional manner
- Argues effectively
- Has a positive self-concept
- Is a caring manager
- Understands the corporate vision
- Is empowered
- Appreciates the importance of safety
- Is a patient listener
- Has effective communication skills
- Is a participative manager
- Projects a professional image
- Is marketing oriented

- Provides quality service
- Is profit minded

Of course, there's nothing wrong with these expressions when they are used in everyday conversation. They become a problem only when it is important to do something about them—when it is important to actually achieve the condition or state implied by the fuzzy. At that point the danger is in using words that don't provide the information that people may need for learning what they are expected to actually do.

Is that risky? You'll have to be the judge of that. But why take any risk at all when you can use a procedure for avoiding the risk?

If you know how to dissect abstractions into the specific performances that say what they mean, you will gain another powerful technique for getting results. Here's a procedure, called goal *analysis*, that will be worth your while to learn. It won't take long.

GOAL ANALYSIS

The purpose of goal analysis is to reduce the likelihood that you will be misinterpreted, and to increase the likelihood that you will get what you want from trainers (or anyone else). It's a short, five-step procedure that ends with a description of the things that people would have to do or say or produce for you to be willing to point to them and say, "Now there's a self-starter" (or whatever the goal may be).

Why is this procedure called goal analysis? Because the word *goal* usually describes broad or general statements of intent (for example, "We want people to be empowered"), and *objective* describes specific (measurable) statements of intent (for example, "We want people to report safety hazards when they encounter them").

WHEN TO DO IT

Carry out a goal analysis (either by yourself or with the help of your trainers) when you find yourself thinking about a situation in terms of fuzzies—for example, if you find yourself thinking:

"They've got an attitude problem" or

"I need to get them motivated to..." or

"They need to appreciate our safety policy."

None of these statements says anything about human performances or about the outcomes those performances are expected to achieve. None of them is observable or measurable. If it's important to achieve the goals, they need to be translated into their performance components. Words like *know* and *understand* are useless for this purpose. They simply are not specific enough to denote, or even to imply, what it is that people are expected to do.

Trainers find that they have to do goal analyses all the time, because people go to them with important problems that they can describe only in abstract terms. "I need you to fix their attitude" is a common request, as is "They need to be more motivated." When trainers get these kinds of requests, they have no choice but to work with the client to determine the meaning behind the fuzzies; it's either that or decide for themselves what they think their client has in mind.

HOW TO DO IT

If this is your first contact with this procedure, you'll learn it faster if you write your thoughts on paper the first time through. Once you've gotten the hang of it, you'll find yourself doing it in your head automatically whenever you hear someone utter an abstraction. (You may also become a little impatient with people who don't know how to do it.)

Before we run through the procedure, there's one thing you need to know. The objective of this procedure is not to hunt for some sort of cosmic, universal definition of abstract statements. The objective is merely to find out what you mean by the goal (abstraction), or what you think it should mean in your particular environment. Having said that, here's how to do it.

State the fuzzy (in terms of outcomes rather than process). Use any words you want; just make sure they describe the end result you are looking for rather than the process for achieving it. (It doesn't make sense to talk about the process for getting there until we know where *there* is.)

Instead of saying:	**Say:**
Develop a responsible attitude.	*Have* a responsible attitude.
Learn to appreciate customers.	*Appreciate* customers.
Become a good leader.	*Be* a good leader.

This may appear to be a small distinction, but it is an important one. If you allow yourself to state your goal in terms of process, you will get tangled up in thinking about how to get there before you know where you're going.

List the performances that define the fuzzy. This is where some garden variety brainstorming is useful. Ask yourself: "What would someone have to do or say or accomplish to make me say that that person has reached the goal?" In other words, answer the question: "How will you know one when you see one?" Jot down your thoughts on a piece of paper, without regard to wording or order.

Don't organize what you write, and don't worry about complete sentences or duplications. Just say what things would be like if the situation were already as you'd like it. Here are some examples of the performances you might jot down:

- Gets reports in on time.

- Writes contracts.

- Smiles when addressing customers.

- Asks for the sale.

- Assembles the widgets without error.

- Drafts five-year plans.

- Keeps work station uncluttered.

- Locks safe when leaving the area.

- Informs co-workers of malfunctions.

- Keeps sales spreadsheets up to date.

I recall a group of police administrators who said it was important that the officers "be professional." Everyone agreed on that. What they didn't agree on was what "be professional" meant in terms of performance. A goal analysis solved the problem. The surprise came when it was discovered that the performances defining this goal were different for police officers than they were for administrators. To the administrators, "be professional" meant that the police officer:

- Dresses sharply

- Is polite to civilians

- Takes control of a traffic situation

To the officers themselves, however, a professional was "someone they would be willing to have as a partner on a dangerous assignment." These were two distinctly different meanings of the same expression. Only when the meanings were revealed was it possible to take intelligent action that got them more of the performance they were looking for.

Sort the list. Once you've jotted down as many items as you can that describe the performances by which you will recognize accomplishment of your goal (remember, you're not looking for some sort of cosmic definition here), take another look at the list. It's likely that some of the items on the list are about as fuzzy as the terms you started with. Never mind. It almost always works that way. You're thinking your way through this issue, and sometimes it takes a little time.

So take a second look at your list and mark any items that are too abstract to be measurable. Can those items be scratched from your list? If you think those items have some important part of the meaning you are searching for, do the same thing with each of them that you did with the fuzzy you started with. In other words, do a mini–goal analysis on each item and ask yourself how you would recognize the goal if you see it. Keep doing that until all of the items on your list are either performances or products of performances.

Write complete sentences. You're almost done. To make sure you have a grasp of the limits of the performances that define your goal, stretch each of the performances into a complete sentence. For example, suppose your list of performances contains the phrase, "Wears safety equipment." When you get to this step you would simply expand that phrase into a complete sentence—possibly like this:

"Machinists wear safety goggles whenever operating the machines in the machine shop."

A complete sentence will help you describe the limits of the performances you are looking for, while at the same time providing more information about what you mean by the abstraction you started with.

Test to see whether you are finished. The final step is simply to make sure you have all of the pieces that matter to you. Look at your list of performances and ask youself, "If someone did or said these things (or refrained from doing or saying these things), would I be willing to say that my goal has been accomplished?" In other words, would you be willing to say that that person represents the state or condition of interest to you? If so, you are finished. If not, there are one or more performances missing from your list.

Don't be alarmed if your list is short. It often works out that way. The fuzzy we start with often sounds as though it has deep, profound meaning, but when we complete a quick goal analysis we sometimes find that the entire meaning can be described in a sentence or two.

I once worked with some people in the oil business who said it was important for stevedores working along the docks to have a "proper spill-prevention attitude." They said it was important not to spill oil into the water or onto the land. To discover what a "proper spill-prevention attitude" meant, we completed a goal analysis. When we were finished, we found that a single sentence would suffice in defining the goal:

"Stevedores follow prescribed operating procedures."

Is it possible to tell whether someone is or isn't following prescribed operating procedures? Of course. The procedures followed by the stevedores were already written down, so it was not difficult to observe proper and improper performance. In other instances, you might end up with a list of six or seven performances (rarely more than ten).

AN EXAMPLE

It is common for managers to want their people to be safety conscious, but it is much less common for them to say what they expect their people to do to warrant that label. But if safety-consciousness is important, it is also important to make the performance expectations equally clear, because the meaning of this abstraction will be different in one department than in another.

When one manager completed a goal analysis on this fuzzy, he was able to tell people, "I want my people to be safety conscious. Now, in my department that means that they need to be able to wear their safety equipment when working with hazardous chemicals. It means they need to be able to recognize safety hazards and know how to report them. It also means that they need to be able to keep the floor around their equipment free of debris, and the aisles free of obstructions. To summarize, I want my people to:

a. Wear safety equipment when appropriate.

b. Be able to recognize safety hazards.

c. Report safety hazards.

d. Keep their work areas free of obstructions and dangerous materials."

With this kind of guidance, the trainers (and you) can make intelligent decisions about what to do next. If they know their business, they may think it through something like this:

- Do these workers already know how to put on and take off their safety equipment? The experienced ones do, but the new hires have to learn how to use the radiation suits. So that's one thing we'll have to teach them.

- Do they already know how to recognize safety hazards that exist in this department? Yes and no. We'll need to make sure they can, so we'll suggest putting that into the instruction.

- Do they know how to report safety hazards? Not anymore. The reporting procedure was just changed, and everyone will have to be taught the new procedure.

- Do they know how to sweep the floor and keep from dumping junk into the aisles? Yes, they all know how to do that. If they aren't doing it, of course, we'll do a performance analysis to find out why. Whatever the reason, that little problem won't be solved by training.

- So we'll recommend some instruction on the first three topics but not on the fourth. If workers aren't keeping their work areas clear of obstructions and dangerous material, we'll offer to take a look at the situation (that is, do a performance analysis) and make a recommendation.

Until you know what safety consciousness means, about all you can do is to hang up safety posters (a colorful but ineffective solution), or to exhort. Unfortunately, exhortation is probably the least effective way to change behavior. In the absence of specific guidance, what would you imagine the training to entail? Lectures on the history of safety? War stories about costly accidents from the past? Poster coloring? It may all be interesting and fun, but it wouldn't increase the amount of safety-conscious performance that you would generate.

ANOTHER EXAMPLE

Some employees of a large bank were concerned that the bank project a "socially responsible" image. Their manager, a bit weary of their finger-pointing condemnation of the behavior of others, gathered them together for a goal analysis session. Having told them that he, too, was interested in social responsibility, he asked them to provide more specific guidance about what actions the bank might take to accomplish this worthy (if ambiguous) goal.

The group warmed to their task and began by filling the air with clouds of meaningless words, accompanied by their habitual finger pointing at "them." As they were guided to follow the goal analysis procedure, however, something rather interesting happened: The fingers began to bend and soon were pointing back at the employees themselves, as a direct result of their own deliberations. This was because they found themselves defining the socially responsible bank as one where (in part):

- Employees come to work on time.

- Employees are prepared to provide the services their customers ask for.

- Customers are greeted promptly when entering the bank and, if needed, are directed to the person who can be of assistance.

- Employees are treated equitably.

- Employees are competent at their assigned tasks.

- Bank resources are allocated toward addressing social or community problems.

Once these and other key components of the term *socially responsible* were ferreted out, it was possible to focus attention on each item separately. It was possible to collect baseline information to answer the question, "How're we doing?" and to determine what actions might lead to improvements.

APPLYING THE POWER

Once you have identified the performances and/or outcomes that define a goal, three things will happen. First, you no longer will need to rely on the fuzzy as a means of communicating an intent. If you wish, you can dispose of the fuzzy words that described the goal and simply show people the list of performances and/or results you want accomplished. This list will offer a clear prescription for action when you say, "Here is what needs to be done to accomplish the goal of _____ ."

Second, you can focus your attention on each of the performances or outcomes and then decide what to do to get more of it. If you discover that one or more of the performances aren't happening to expectation, you can carry out a performance analysis for each item. (The next chapter will show you how.) That will tell you what is causing the faulty performance and suggest remedies to correct it.

Third, you can actually chart your progress toward accomplishment of the goal, no matter how abstract or intangible it first appeared. This is done by charting progress toward the accomplishment of each of the important performances. For example, if a goal analysis shows that the item *security consciousness* means, in part, that people do not leave sensitive documents unattended, you can chart either the number of instances in which violations were discovered or the number of instances in which there were no violations. (The latter is a more positive approach.) These simple charts might look like the following graph. (Notice that the vertical scale is reversed so that the curve moves *upward* as progress is made.)

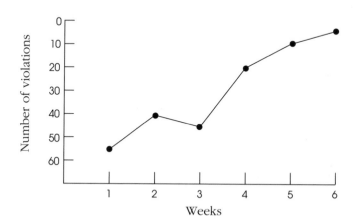

Charts are a way of informing people about what is considered important; people tend to do those things that will make the charts look good.

SUMMARY

Complete a goal analysis whenever there is an important outcome to accomplish that you or someone else can describe only in general or abstract terms (fuzzies). To carry out the analysis:

- Describe your goal in terms of outcomes rather than in terms of process.

- Identify what someone would have to do or say or accomplish for you to be willing to say the outcome (goal) has been achieved. (Sometimes any one of several different actions would let you say your goal has been achieved.)

- Sort the list. Identify remaining fuzzies and replace them with the performances that say what they mean.

- Write a complete sentence describing each of the performances on your final list.

- Test to make sure you have all of the components that are important to you.

For more information about this technique, and for more examples, read *Goal Analysis* (see Useful Resources, page 147). In addition, call the trainers and ask them to arrange a short workshop on goal analysis for the managers and supervisors of your department or division. It will be time well spent.

WHERE WE'RE HEADED

With the goal analysis in hand, you are ready to develop a form of X-ray vision that will give you the power to decide which action will solve your human performance problems. This is a key tool that should be at the fingertips of every manager. It's a tool you can't afford to do without.

4

How to Solve Performance Problems

People don't usually say that they have an "aspirin problem" when they have a headache, or that they have a "compressed air problem" when they have a flat tire, or that they have a "hammer problem" when they find a nail that needs pounding. The *problems* (things that need fixing) are the headache, the flat tire, and the nail; the *solutions* are the aspirin, the compressed air, and the hammering. But for some reason most managers claim they have a "training problem" when something else isn't happening to their satisfaction. And once they've said they have a training problem, they almost always conclude that they need a training solution. They're often wrong, and when they are wrong, it means they've selected a solution that won't solve whatever their real problem may be.

The way to avoid this expensive (and often embarrassing) trap is to learn to recognize the difference between problems and solutions related to human performance, and to learn a procedure for matching the solutions to the problems. You already know how to do that in the area of your specialty, and it isn't difficult to learn to do it with human performance, either. It just takes a little thought and a little practice. This chapter will show you how. We'll begin with the difference between problems and solutions.

SOLUTIONS ARE NOT PROBLEMS

Problems occur when things don't happen to your satisfaction. The "problem" is some indication that there is a gap between what is actually happening and what you expect to happen; a solution is a way to eliminate that gap. Problems might be expressed as follows:

- My salespeople don't have the right attitude about customers.
- This weld is too raggedy.
- These truck drivers are having too many accidents.

Solutions, on the other hand, are actions that may be taken to correct the problems. Solutions might be expressed as follows:

- My salespeople will complete the course on customer courtesy.
- These welders will be given further training in welding.
- We'll analyze the data to find out why our drivers are having so many accidents.

With this distinction in mind, you can see the trap in a comment such as, "I've got a training problem." There's no such thing. Training is a solution, not a problem. Training is what you do to get rid of a problem, such as a lack of skill or knowledge. But there are many reasons why people don't perform at their best, reasons not remedied by training.

- They've forgotten how to do it.

- They don't know what's expected of them.

- They don't have the authority to do it.

- They don't get timely information (feedback) about how well they're doing.

- Their information sources (documentation) are poorly designed, inaccessible, or nonexistent.

- Their work station is clumsily designed.

- They're punished or ignored for doing it right.

- They're rewarded for doing it wrong.

- Nobody ever notices whether they do it right or not.

- Their organization makes desired performance difficult or impossible.

Unfortunately, when some managers notice someone performing inadequately, there is a tendency to conclude that they've "got a training problem." But this approach opens the door to all sorts of mischief. If you say that to a trainer who doesn't know the craft, he or she probably will begin building a course, without really addressing the problem first. You might then find yourself with a fine, entertaining course that trainees rave about but that doesn't do any good. Or, you might find yourself with a course that uses lots of shiny, expensive hardware but that doesn't solve the problem.

If someone says "I've got a training problem" to trainers who do know their craft, those trainers will say to themselves, "Hmm. Here's someone who doesn't know the difference between problems and solutions. The first thing I need to do is to find out what event is causing this person to conclude that training is needed." The trainer will then begin tactfully to ask questions intended to discover what the problem is, so that he or she can determine whether training should be part or all of the solution. In other words, the trainer will begin to carry out a performance analysis. Unless someone diagnoses the problems before settling on solutions, the problems either won't get solved or will be attacked with solutions that won't work. To put it bluntly, trainers have to know how to do diagnoses because most managers don't.

Managers who do know how to match solutions to performance problems won't demand training that isn't necessary. The ability to carry out a performance analysis therefore will substantially increase your power to improve performance. This chapter will prepare you to carry out performance analyses.

WHAT IS A PERFORMANCE ANALYSIS?

A performance analysis is a procedure for matching solutions to problems in human performance. It begins by identifying the difference(s) between actual and desired performance, then identifies the cause(s) of the discrepancy, and finally suggests courses of action to address those causes. The analysis is carried out by answering a sequence of questions. Usually, the analysis of a performance discrepancy takes no longer than a few minutes. When it takes longer it is only because information needed to answer questions is not immediately available.

Read through the Checklist on the following page before going on to the explanation of how to use it.

PERFORMANCE ANALYSIS CHECKLIST

1   **Whose performance is at issue?**

2   **What is the performance discrepancy?**
a. What is actually happening?
b. What should be happening?

3   **What is the approximate cost of the discrepancy?**
(What would happen if you ignored the problem?)

4   **Is the discrepancy a skill deficiency?**
(Are they unable to do it?)

5   **Yes...it *is* a skill deficiency:**
a. Can the job or task be simplified?
b. Are the tasks performed often?
c. Will other factors impede performance?

6   **No...it is *not* a skill deficiency:**
a. Are the performers being *punished* for doing it right?
b. Are the performers being *rewarded* for doing it wrong?
c. Are there no *consequences* at all to the performer for performing, either right or wrong?
d. Are there *obstacles* to performing as expected?

7   **List the causes of the discrepancy.**

8   **Describe solutions.**

9   **Estimate the cost of each solution.**

10   **Select the cost-effective solutions that can be implemented (those that are practical to implement).**

11   **Implement the solutions.**

WHEN TO USE IT

Use the performance analysis whenever you feel that there is a difference between what workers actually do and what they should be doing. Use it whenever you find yourself thinking thoughts such as these:

They're not doing what they should be doing.

They're not getting the results they should be getting.

They're not properly motivated to_____.

They need training.

They don't have the right attitude about_____.

Their reports are always late.

They don't make enough sales calls.

THE PROCEDURE

You have already read through the Performance Analysis Checklist on page 51. To aid your understanding, there is a fold-out version of this Checklist at the back of the book. Fold the Checklist out, and keep it in front of you as a reference as you work through the procedure explanations that follow.

1. Decide whose performance is at issue. This analysis is of no value in the abstract. Therefore, identify whose performance is at issue. It might be a person, or a group of people in a single category. For example, at issue might be the performance of a truck driver, a production manager, or a lathe operator. Or it might be that there is a problem with the performance of all of the drivers, the entire sales staff, or the assemblers in Department X. Be sure to identify the performers at issue before proceeding.

2. Describe the discrepancy. Describe the actual performance and the desired performance. State what it is that someone is doing that he or she shouldn't be doing; or state what the person is not doing that he or she should be doing. Then state what the desired performance should be. The description must be in terms of performance, in terms of doing. Abstract (fuzzy) language just doesn't communicate your desires. Your knowledge of goal analysis will make this step easier to complete. Here are some examples of good and bad descriptions:

Bad: They're not motivated.

Good: They're not getting their reports in on time.

Bad: They don't have the right attitude toward customers.

Good: They're not answering the telephone within two rings.

Bad: They're not conscientious enough.

Good: Their production is 10 percent below expectation.

Bad: They're not safety conscious.

Good: They leave boxes stacked in the aisles.

The differences between what should be happening and what is actually happening might be described like this:

Actual: Reports are up to three weeks late.

Desired: Reports are submitted by deadline.

Actual: Half of the incoming calls are not answered until the fourth or fifth ring.

Desired: Phones should be answered within two rings.

Actual: Their production is 10 percent below expectation.

Desired: Their production should match or exceed
         expectation.

Actual: Boxes are stacked in traffic lanes at least twice
         each day, causing a traffic hazard.

Desired: Boxes should always be stacked in designated
         areas.

3. Estimate the size (cost) of the discrepancy. How much
is this problem costing you? What would happen if you ignored it? Is it slowing down production, taking up your time,
irritating and possibly losing customers? Is it causing accidents? Does it result in materials waste? Consider all of the
consequences of the discrepancy and estimate an approximate
cost. Until you estimate the cost of the problem you will be
in no position to select a solution that costs less than the
problem.

   If you have difficulty estimating the cost, imagine that
someone has challenged you by saying, "Look. That problem
is so trivial it isn't worth doing anything about." How would
you respond? If you can't point to one or more serious consequences (costs) caused by the performance discrepancy,
maybe it *is* too small to bother with.

4. Decide whether the discrepancy is a skill deficiency.
Do the workers already know how to do it the way you want
it done? Could they perform the way you want them to perform if their lives depended on it? If they can't do it, then
training is likely to be part or all of the solution. If, on the
other hand, they already can do what is expected of them
but for some reason aren't doing it, then there is no skill
deficiency. In this case, training is unlikely to be required, and
the next step will be to determine why workers aren't doing
what they already know how to do. If you aren't sure
whether people can now do what they should be doing, the
simplest move is to ask them.

5. Yes...it is a skill deficiency. They cannot now perform the way you want them to. If they couldn't perform as desired if their lives depended on it—then it may be that they need training. But hold on. There's more to consider before rushing off to the training store. As you have seen from Chapter 3, there are a number of remedies that might get you where you want to go, so answer these questions before concluding that training is the answer.

    a. Can the job be simplified? Sometimes it is possible to simplify or redesign a job or task and therefore reduce or eliminate the need for training. Sometimes this can be done by creating checklists or other job aids. Sometimes it can be done by changing the scope of the job itself. If the job can be simplified, keep that in mind as a possible solution. Here are two examples:

Example: When the controls on a large machine were clearly labeled, the operating errors disappeared, along with a need for training.

Example: When a checklist of items to be inspected was given to the inspectors, they no longer failed to check critical items, and the need for training was eliminated.

    b. Are the tasks performed often? If so and people still aren't performing to your satisfaction, it is likely that they aren't getting information (feedback) about the quality of their performance. When a task is performed often and still isn't being done to satisfaction, introducing feedback is likely to be the solution.

Example: When inspectors of incoming raw materials were provided with a gauge against which to compare their inspection of material smoothness, their inspection accuracy immediately improved and no additional training was needed.

Example: When a mirror was placed behind the telephone of a sour-sounding telephone operator, he could see when he wasn't smiling. This simple feedback device eliminated the need to "teach" him to smile when answering the phone.

Example: It is common practice to train salespeople and then to send them out into their territories to sell. Sometimes, however, it is impractical to send a coach along during the first few critical weeks of on-the-job practice of the newly learned selling skills. When this happens, there may be consequences for good performance (a sale is made) or poor performance (no sale is made, or worse, the customer is driven away), but there is no guidance (feedback) to identify those aspects of the performance in need of correction or improvement. When this happens, bad habits develop quickly.

If the skill is not performed often, the remedies to think about are practice and job aids. Remember, you can't store training. So when skills are used only once in a while, either arrange for periodic skills practice or have trainers create job aids that will remind people of what to do when it comes time to do it. On occasion, both remedies may be in order.

Although remedies such as job simplification, job aids, feedback, and practice are often useful for avoiding training, there is no reason why you should have to become expert yourself at applying these interventions. That's what your trainers and other human factors people are for. You merely need to know that these remedies exist and that they will save you time and money when they can be used. They are almost always less expensive than the training solution.

   c. Will other factors impede performance? You are dealing with a performance discrepancy—they simply don't know how to do it the way they're expected to. But what will happen when they *do* learn to do it right? Will skill be enough to guarantee performance? Or will other factors interfere? To make sure you collect *all* the clues that will lead you to the solutions to your problem, go now to item #6 on the Performance Analysis Checklist. Pretend that the non-performers have just learned to do what they need to do, and that you are looking for additional reasons why performance may be impeded.

6. No...it is not a skill deficiency. They can perform the way you want them to but aren't doing so. You need to find out why they aren't doing what they *already know how to do*. There are four main reasons why people don't do what they know how to do.

- They are being punished for doing it right.

- They are being rewarded for doing it in some undesired way.

- They are ignored for doing it, *right or wrong.*

- There are obstacles that prevent them from doing it.

There are hundreds of ways to create an upside-down consequence environment, one in which desired performance is punished and/or ignored, or in which undesired performance is rewarded. Some are blatant and some are subtle.

Example: The maintenance staff was instructed by management to conduct a preventive maintenance routine on any piece of equipment they worked on. But many technicians were not following instructions, and someone thought they needed their attitudes adjusted. Training was suggested. But those who did take the time to conduct the desired preventive maintenance routines had to report longer MTTRs (Mean Times to Repair). In other words, they took longer on a troubleshooting call than those who skipped the preventive maintenance routine. Consequently, their speedier colleagues tended to get the raises and promotions.

Example: Even though she's number 12 on the mail delivery route in the marketing department, Marcia always gets her mail first. Why? It's because she always has a smile and a jolly word for the mail boy, who is usually ignored or growled at by the other department staff.

Example: Uncle Willie says, "I don't go to church anymore. My mother started me going when I was quite young. But the pews were hard, and they never talked about anything I understood. The statues scared the heck out of me, and no matter what I did, people glared at me and told me to shush. When I got a little older I realized that most of the time they were telling me how bad I was. So I don't go back."

Example: You are having a dinner party. While the kids are playing quietly in the corner (desired performance), you ignore them. When they act up (undesired performance), you turn your attention upon them and tell them to pipe down. Although you may think you are punishing them with your threats, it is more likely that you are rewarding them with your attention. You may wonder why the children keep doing what you've told them to stop doing. But if you're fanning the fire (by heaping attention on the unwanted behavior), you shouldn't wonder that it won't go out.

You probably can think of many more instances in which the desired performance was either punished or ignored, or in which other-than-desired performance was rewarded. Although topsy-turvy consequences can pose huge obstacles to performance, the problem is usually easy to correct.

It is important to note that we don't have any choice over whether we are going to influence performance through the application of consequences (rewards and punishments). We influence performance whether we like it or not. We do it when we smile, we do it when we frown, we do it when we comment favorably or unfavorably on someone's work. The fact is, each one of us is personally a powerful source of rewards and punishments. Although we can control whether those rewards and punishments work for us or against us, we can't stop dispensing them. So if we accidentally smile on undesired performance, we just may get more of it, regardless of the words we may be saying at the time.

At this point you may be thinking, "I'm not going to reward workers for doing what they get paid to do anyway," or, "I don't have that kind of control over raises and promotions."

These are reasonable thoughts. But, we're not talking about raises and promotions. We're talking about consequences that take place soon after a desired event has occurred. That may mean a smile, a pat on the back, a bit of verbal praise, an entry in a personnel file, a mention in the department monthly report, a party to celebrate a quota achieved, or any number of similar consequences that seldom cost a nickel to apply. We're talking about the little things that say, "You're doing a good job," or, "You're doing a better job today than you did yesterday," or, "You're improving." These are the little things that make a work environment positive rather than punishing.

One of the first steps in this portion of the performance analysis, then, is to identify any topsy-turvy consequences. Ask the following questions:

a. Are the performers being punished for doing it right? First, list all the things that happen to the performers when performing as desired.

Caution: It is tempting here to list consequences for people other than the performer. But it doesn't matter that poor performance causes *you* to be upset, or that it causes *others* extra work; what matters is what happens to the performers in question.

Next, determine whether any of the consequences are considered punishing by the performer. If so, you will have located a cause of the problem.

Caution: It is sometimes easy to confuse consequences that are rewarding to *you* with those that are in fact punishing to others. For example, you may find it very pleasing to be able to reduce someone's budget when that person has performed efficiently, but the performer may consider that very same consequence to be decidedly punishing.

Example: Teachers are expected to help their students learn the subjects being taught. That's the desired performance. Often, however, those teachers who are "too successful" experience punishing consequences. For one thing, they may be accused of "grade inflation" when they give a larger proportion of *A*'s and *B*'s than the normal distribution curve would suggest. For another, they may be accused of giving courses that are too easy. Their accusers don't acknowledge that a higher percentage of good grades might come from good teaching; they simply cast doubt on (punish) teachers who give grades that do not conform to the usual standard. (How long would your company stay in business if policy insisted that only 70 per cent of the products "passed" before leaving the plant?) Under such circumstance, it is difficult for teachers to stay interested in continued teaching success.

When desired performance leads to punishment the frequency of the desired performance will decrease. Simply put, people tend to spend their time doing those things that make their world brighter. The remedy here is to find one or more ways to reward, rather than punish, people for doing things the way you say you want them done.

b. Are the performers being rewarded for doing it wrong? First, list all the things that happen *to the performers* when they perform in a way *other* than what is expected. Again, make sure you list only those consequences that directly affect the performers. Then, decide whether any of those consequences are considered rewarding by the performers. If they are, you will have located another cause of the problem. (If you're not sure, the fastest thing to do is to ask a performer.) The solution will be to remove the source of reward for undesired performance.

Example:

Who?	Secretarial assistants.
Desired Performance?	They should complete work in a timely manner.
Actual performance?	They take too long to do the work.
Skill deficiency?	No.
Consequences of undesired performance?	Someone else completes the work.
Remedy?	Require that assistants do their own work, thereby allowing them to experience the consequences of their own actions.

When undesired performance (slow work) leads to a rewarding situation (somebody else will do the work), there is no reason for the performer to want to do it differently. The remedy here is to make the assistants' world dimmer rather than brighter when the work isn't up to expectations.

c. Are there no consequences at all to the performer for performing, either right or wrong? Sometimes all hell breaks loose when someone doesn't perform in the desired way, but none of the "hell" lands on the performer. If the consequences for either good or poor performance don't affect the performer *directly,* chances are that desired performance won't continue for very long. When, from the performer's point of view, there are no consequences for either desired or undesired performance, it shouldn't surprise anyone when "doing it the desired way" takes on a low priority for the performer.

Example: At one company, it was common practice to pump music and radio commercials into the ears of customers who phoned in and were put on hold. Some of the customers decided to take their business elsewhere. So the company did experience consequences. But those customers didn't tell anyone they were leaving. Since no direct consequences were experienced by the persons who initiated the hostile practice, it was continued, and even more customers left.

Example: A high school principal once told me of his victory with litter. "Litter is a real eyesore at our school because we have a concrete courtyard—no bushes to throw things into, you see. So I tried everything to get the kids to stop littering. First, I went on the school's public address system and exhorted. Then I cajoled. I even threatened. But nothing seemed to work. Finally, I did a performance analysis, and realized that while there were lots of consequences resulting from the litter—the parents complained, the school board complained, trash collection costs increased, and I was laughed at by my colleagues—none of those consequences hit the students themselves. So I plunked a big dumpster into the middle of our courtyard and told the kids that when it was filled with litter we'd have a party. Did it work? Hey, not only did they stop littering, they began bringing trash from home!"

Example: At some companies, the primary response to an increase in accident rates is to hang up additional safety posters, and to hold meetings during which the importance of safety is emphasized. Although such activities may serve as a reminder to all, the accident rate cannot be expected to decrease unless consequences are arranged for those actually causing the accidents. A shower of let's-think-safety activities sprinkled on everyone won't work nearly as well as a focused stream of let's-improve-*your*-performance directed at those causing the problems.

d. Are there obstacles to doing it right? Check to see if the performers have the opportunity to do what you expect of them. Check at least for these obstacles:

- Do workers know what is expected of them?
- Do they have permission (authority) to perform?
- Do they have the time to perform?
- Do they have the tools and equipment needed?
- Do they have adequate space to perform?
- Is their workplace conducive to performing?
- Are they allowed to interact with those who have an impact on their work?

Example: A computer technician was found to be damaging as many computers as he was repairing, although the damage often was not noticed until some time after the computers were returned to their owners. In the process of making repairs, he was producing static electricity, which damaged some of the computer chips. When the technician was provided with—and was required to use—a grounding strap, he ceased to damage the computer chips. The absence of a grounding strap was the obstacle. Removing the obstacle solved the problem. No training was required.

7. List the causes of the discrepancy. List the causes suggested by your answers to the previous questions. For example, if there are obstacles, list the obstacles to be removed. If some of the consequences for desired performance are punishing, list the punishing consequences.

8. Describe the solutions. Beside each of the causes you have listed, describe a suitable remedy. Try to be specific. Rather than simply writing "remove punishment," describe how you will do that.

Example: The manager of a corporate video department was concerned that his graphic artist never seemed to get his work finished by the deadline. A short performance analysis revealed that there was an obstacle to meeting deadlines: the artist had too much artwork to do as favors for other managers. Once the obstacle was discovered, the video manager devised a policy that required payment for all artwork done by his department. When managers discovered that they would have to pay for the artwork they were accustomed to getting free, they stopped making private demands on the artist's time. When the video manager completed his performance analysis, the main points looked something like this:

Performance discrepancy?	The graphic artist doesn't get assignments done on time.
Cost?	About $50,000 per year, due to missed deadlines.
Skill deficiency?	No. He could do it if he really had to.
Obstacles?	High demand for personal favors by other managers (much of which was considered nuisance work).
Remedy?	Initiate and publicize a policy requiring payment for all artwork previously requested as favors, and schedule the work to respect the artist's deadlines.

9. Estimate the cost of each solution. Write the estimate beside the solution. This step usually takes only a few seconds to complete, because the cost of most solutions will be negligible.

> **Example:**   In the example of the graphic artist described above, the cost of drafting and disseminating the new policy was estimated to be $500, including the manager's time.

10. Select the solutions. Because you know the approximate cost of the problem and the cost of the solutions, it is usually easy to select the most cost-effective solution or combination of solutions. This is especially so when you involve others in planning the solutions. Select the least expensive solution(s) that address the problem (from among those that cost less than the problem) and that are practical—those that you actually have the authority to apply. It won't help, for example, to describe a solution that states, "A new corporate policy will _____," if you don't have any chance of getting such a policy written and implemented. Stay with solutions that you can actually manage.

Check to make sure that you have a solution that will address each of the problems you identified during the analysis.

11. Implement the solutions. Put the solutions into practice, and then monitor the situation to see how well the solutions are working. Your action plan should include a description of your intended outcome (what things will be like when your solutions have worked). The plan should also list the steps for accomplishing the outcome.

The above description of the analysis procedure may lead you to think that a performance analysis takes a long time to complete. Not true. Most of the time a performance analysis will take only a short time to complete, and the solution will take only a little of your time to implement. The wise course of action is to get your trainers to help you with the analysis of any performance problem that you can't solve in a few minutes.

SUMMARY

Here is a summary of the problems and solutions portion of the analysis. It can be used as a reminder of the classes of solutions that are most often indicated for the problems shown. This summary is repeated as the Performance Problem Solution Checklist for handy reference in Chapter 9.

PROBLEMS	**SOLUTIONS**

They *can't* do it, and...

the skill is used often:	• Provide feedback
	• Simplify the task.
the skill is used rarely:	• Provide job aids to prompt desired performance.
	• Simplify the job.
	• Provide periodic practice.
	(Training will be required if the above remedies are inadequate.)

They *can* do it, but...

doing it right leads to punishment:	• Remove the sources of punishment.
doing it wrong is more satisfying:	• Remove the rewards for incorrect performance.
nobody notices when they do it right:	• Apply consequences to the performer for doing it right.
there are obstacles to performing as desired:	• Remove the obstacles (or help people work around them).

For a more complete explanation of the analysis procedure and a more extensive collection of examples, you might want to read *Analyzing Performance Problems* (see Useful Resources, page 147). It would also be appropriate to ask your trainers to conduct a short workshop on this technique for all managers in your department. Knowing how to use this tool can save you literally thousands, and sometimes millions, of dollars.

Warning: When you are able to do a performance analysis, you will be able to see at a glance if a wrong solution is being proposed—or applied. Once that happens you may need to struggle to maintain your tactful posture.

WHERE WE'RE HEADED

There's one more thing to do before bearding the trainers in their dens. And that is to peek behind the scenes of a training department populated by trainers experienced at applying the basic techniques of the technologies. A brief look at what they do will help you negotiate for the services you need.

5

How the Magic
Goes In

To get the services you need, it is useful to have at least some idea of what the state-of-the-art training department does.

"Wait a minute," I hear you shouting. "I don't want to know how our accountants count their beans, and I don't want to know how the trainers write their lesson plans, either." Fair enough. But a quick look at what they do, rather than a dissertation on how they do it, will prepare you to respond to the kinds of questions you may be asked when you ask for services. It will help you understand why they may want to observe competent performers at work. It will help show you how the entire training enterprise differs from the stand-up-and-tell-'em days. And it will help you identify trainers who are unlikely to produce the results you need—before you invest time and money in a project.

PROCESSING A TRAINING REQUEST

Let's look behind the scenes to see what might happen in an up-to-date training department when training is requested. The department we'll visit is populated by performance-oriented trainers who are skilled at providing both training and non-training services, and they are concerned that everything they set out to do will add value to the organization. So, when trainers receive a request for their services, they will follow the key steps outlined below, regardless of what those steps happen to be called in any given shop. Because trainers have to live within a variety of constraints (like everyone else), there are times when they may not have the luxury of completing all of the steps. Given the opportunity, however, here is how a training request might be processed. These steps are highlighted in the chart on page 84.

Verify the training need. The first step is always to verify that the remedy (intervention) will be useful in solving the problem that stimulated the request. There are a number of analysis tools available, and the trainers will use whichever is appropriate to the situation.

Suppose you were to eavesdrop on a training analyst and a manager during this step in the process. You might hear the following sort of conversation between them:

Manager: I need a course to teach my phone solicitors to be more polite to customers.

Analyst: All right. Can you tell me what they aren't doing that they should be doing?

Manager: Well, for one thing, they put customers on hold for longer than they're supposed to.

Analyst: I see. Anything else?

Manager:	Yes. They're sometimes rude to the callers.
Analyst:	Do they know how to be polite? That is, do they know how *not* to be rude?
Manager:	Sure they do! They've all had the training that certified their customer relations skills. But they're not doing it.

At this point the analyst is probably thinking, ""It looks as though these workers already know how to do what's expected of them, so we don't have a situation that can be solved by training. I've got to find out why these people aren't doing what they already know how to do so that I can suggest an appropriate fix." Sounds familiar, right? You no doubt recognized this as part of a performance analysis.

Back at the ranch...the analyst might have a conversation with the training manager that would sound like this:

Analyst:	I talked with Lotta Smarts about some training.
Training Manager:	And?
Analyst:	She doesn't need training. Her people already know how to perform the way she wants them to.
Training Manager:	Did you verify?
Analyst:	Yes. They perform correctly at least half the time. That confirms that they already know how to perform.
Training Manager:	How firm is she?
Analyst:	Well, she's pretty set on having some training, and she's already convinced her boss to provide a budget.

Training Manager:	Length?
Analyst:	She's set on a two-day course.
Training Manager:	Ouch! Will she modify?
Analyst:	I think so. She's bright, and once she sees a graphic summary of the situation, I think she'll see she doesn't need training.
Training Manager:	So are you drafting a situation summary?
Analyst:	Yes. It will show that she should be able to solve the problem for about five percent of what the training would cost. That'll make her look good when she shows it to her manager. I'm convinced they'll both go for the feedback solution I've described to her.

Decide on a course of action. Having identified the cause of the problem that led to the request for training, the next step is to decide on the solution. Often, the solution is obvious—for example, when new hires are expected to operate equipment they've never seen before. Sometimes the situation requires some discussion with the manager making the request. In the case of the previous example, a part of the discussion might go something like this:

Analyst:	Let me be sure I understand your situation. The only time one of your people finds out that they've been rude is when a caller hangs up or complains. Right?
Manager:	Yes. The supervisor is also taking calls, and she can't always observe everyone else at the same time.

Analyst: So we need to create some sort of "rudeness indicator" so that people will know when their performance is not okay. In other words, we need to provide a source of feedback so they'll know when they're doing it right and when they're doing it wrong.

Manager: What have you got in mind?

The manager and analyst will then discuss a series of options and select a course of action that will be practical and affordable.

THE TRAINING DEVELOPMENT PROCESS

When *training* is needed as part of the pattern of remedies, the following sequence of events will occur. (Don't let the number of steps being described lead you to conclude that the process will take forever, or that it is necessarily costly.)

Derive objectives. Trainers don't begin developing training until they know what that training will be expected to accomplish. They want as clear a picture of the expected outcomes of the training as they can get, just as manufacturing wants a good set of blueprints before turning the manufacturing crank.

So the trainers will engage in whichever analysis procedures are appropriate for determining the important outcomes to be achieved. Sometimes they will be able to do this in their offices. Sometimes, however, they will have to actually observe competent people at work and ask them questions

SAMPLE INSTRUCTIONAL OBJECTIVES

Here are sample objectives from a variety of subjects. Without statements as specific as these to guide development and implementation of the training, you'd have a course without a rudder.

Objective: Given Review Worksheet ZX-3, and one of your subordinates, be able to carry out a performance review.

Criteria: a. All items on the worksheet have been covered.
           b. The employee has agreed to the improvement plan discussed during the review.
           c. The employee was not insulted or demeaned during the review.

Objective: Given a videotape of an emergency situation in a confined space, be able to formulate (write) a rescue plan.

Criteria: The plan must include a description of the number of rescuers and the equipment needed, as well as precautions that must be taken before the rescue is attempted.

Objective: Given a micrometer and a number of items to be measured, be able to measure and record the thickness of each item.

Criterion: Each reading is as accurate as the instrument allows.

Objective: Be able to replace any part in the Sockthief washer.

Criteria: a. The washer operates normally after the part replacement.
           b. No unsafe practices were used.
           c. There is no damage to the washer, equipment, tools, or surrounding area.

Objective: In an interview environment, be able to interview an applicant for employment in your department.

Criteria: a. All information required by Form 23-X has been elicited and the form properly completed.
           b. The interviewee was not insulted or demeaned during the interview.

Objective: Given a Radbuster radiation suit, be able to put it on within five minutes.

Criteria: There is no damage to the suit, and the components of the suit were put on in the order prescribed in the *Really Rad Manual*, 1997.

about what they are doing. This is a task analysis. You will be much more likely to get instruction that has value if you provide the necessary access.

In deriving the objectives, trainers will follow an "audit trail"—somewhat like a trail of breadcrumbs—that leads from the job to the classroom. First, they will describe how competent performers do the task (task analyses), so that they will have a picture of what the trainees will be expected to do when they are competent.

Trainers will then draft objectives to describe the outcomes that the instruction should accomplish. Only when these objectives have been drafted will they be ready for the next steps. (Sample instructional objectives are shown on the page opposite.)

Describe the training audience. Somewhere along the way the developers will draft a comprehensive description of the target audience. This is to make it possible to tailor the instruction to the people for whom it will be intended. The description will influence the choice of language and examples, and the level at which the material is prepared. For example, if the intended audience finds reading difficult, the reading load will be minimized by the way the page is designed or the screen laid out, by the use of video, or by the use of instructors or other trainees.

Draft skill hierarchies. After drafting the objectives, the developers will draft one or more skill hierarchies. This tool looks like an organization chart, except that it depicts skills rather than organizational functions.

The skill hierarchy is useful because it shows which skills are independent of one another (that is, can be learned in any order), and which are dependent (that is, must be learned in a specific order). It is important to have a picture of these

A SAMPLE SKILL HIERARCHY

TERMINAL OBJECTIVE

Given a standard repair ticket, be able to complete the ticket to show charges to be paid by the customer for a repair. Criteria: all charges are correct, no charges are omitted, and the customer is not charged for work not completed.

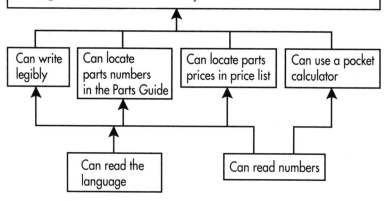

Read the hierarchy from top down, like this:

Before anyone can practice preparing a repair ticket, he or she needs to be able to write legibly, locate part numbers, locate parts prices, and use a pocket calculator. These skills can be learned in any order.

Before learning how to locate part numbers or parts prices, anyone would first need to be able to read the language and read numbers. And, before learning to use a pocket calculator, anyone would need to learn to read numbers. Language reading and number reading can be learned in any order.

The skill hierarchy is useful because it shows which skills are independent of one another (that is, can be learned in any order), and which are dependent (that is, must be learned in a specific order). It also shows how to make efficient use of scarce instructional resources.

relationships when designing instruction because it provides information about where the instruction should begin, about how the lessons should be sequenced, and about how to make use of scarce instructional resources. (An example of a hierarchy is shown on the page opposite.)

Review existing resources. With objectives and a description of the target audience in hand, it is possible to compare them against existing courses, or pieces of courses, that either are currently being offered by your trainers or are available from vendors. This review will prevent duplication of effort. (In other words, developers won't have to reinvent the wheel.) If the needed instruction already exists, and if it looks as though it will do the job, use it. Not only would it be a waste of money to develop what already exists, it would take longer to get the help you need.

Determine the scope of the instruction. At this point a decision will be made regarding the objectives to include in the instruction. Several considerations enter into this decision, such as what the target trainees already know and can do, the amount of time available for the training, the resources that are available, and the lead time available for development.

Draft the skill checks. Before the development process begins, the course developers will draft the means by which the success of the instruction will be measured. It is important that these tools be drafted before the training is developed, to prevent measuring devices from being constructed to measure what was *taught*, rather than whether

SAMPLE SKILL CHECKS

Here are two objectives and skill checks appropriate for measuring their accomplishment. Notice that in each instance, the skill check asks the trainee to do exactly what the objective requires—nothing more, nothing less.

Objective: Given an employment applicant and an Application Interview Summary form, be able to carry out an application interview.

Criteria: a. All items on the summary form have been elicited and entered in the appropriate spaces.
            b. The applicant was not insulted or demeaned during the review.

Skill Check:
1. On the table in video room B, you will find a copy of the Application Interview Summary. Ask another trainee to serve as a job applicant for a job as your assistant.
2. When you are ready, turn on the video equipment and begin your interview.
3. Record the information you elicit in the spaces provided on the summary form.
4. When you have finished the interview, ask a course manager to review the tape with you.

Objective: Given a micrometer and a number of items to be measured, be able to measure and record the thickness of each item.

Criterion: Each reading is as accurate as the instrument allows.

Skill Check:
1. Take your micrometer to station 3 in breakout room A.
2. Measure the thickness (to 0.001 inch) of each of the items you find on the table.
3. Write the thickness of each item on the answer sheet provided.

objectives were accomplished. That's good news for you, because well-designed skill checks (as performance tests are often called) allow trainers to guarantee that trainees will be able to perform as desired before being stamped with a seal of approval. (Sample skill checks and matching objectives are shown on the page opposite.)

Derive the instructional content. With objectives and skill checks in hand, developers will derive the content of the instruction. Content is derived by reviewing the objective and the target population description, and answering the key question, "Why aren't these trainees ready to practice this objective now?" If trainees already know everything they need to know, and only need practice to accomplish the objective, then that lesson will contain only practice and feedback. If, on the other hand, trainees aren't ready to practice because there is something they don't know, or can't do, or because there are dangers they don't yet know how to avoid, the instruction will include whatever is necessary to prepare them to practice safely.

Notice that content derivation is not the first step in the process. The days when trainers would respond to the "Teach them something about…" approach by leaping right into selecting content went the way of the dodo bird. To select content before having a clear picture of the intended results of the instruction is amateurish, ineffective, and a costly way to achieve nonresults.

Select the delivery system. Developers will next decide on the means by which the instruction will be delivered. This decision is delayed until now, however, because the decision will be influenced by the objectives, by the target trainees, by the importance of the training outcomes, and by some other factors. Trainers sometimes moan when they hear someone making a decision about how the instruction will be delivered before they know what the instruction will include. Comments such as, "I want a three-day course, and I want it on video," make about as much sense to professional trainers as, "Let's invent a new product and use drill presses to make them."

Your interest should be in having the instruction delivered by the most economical means that will get you the performance you need. Anything else would be an extravagance. This is where extra caution will pay off, because fads and favorites often exert more influence than sense. Although the selection of a delivery system is one of the simplest decisions in the development process, you may find people on your doorstep with large, multicolored matrices—something like astrological charts—purporting to tell you which items of equipment you will need to buy.

Fortunately, there is a simple way to protect yourself from this abyss. Here's how: Review the objectives you want accomplished (of course, if you don't have any objectives you'll be a dead duck), and put your finger on the words that tell you what the learner will be expected to do or accomplish. You should then be able to make sense of any media proposal presented to you. With your eye on the intended outcomes, you can tell whether the proposed delivery system will provide the simplest, most direct, and least expensive way to provide practice and feedback in the skills to be learned.

Here's an example of how a conversation might go with one of the faddish trainers trying to talk you into more training hardware than you need:

Trainer: So you really should opt for laser-optimized computer-driven instruction for your course.

You: Why?

Trainer: It's the latest thing. And we have some great software that lets us provide maximum interaction with the trainee. It has instant access and can branch the trainees from any point in the instruction to any other point, at the blink of an eye.

You: But look at these objectives you drafted for me. (Pointing to objectives) They say that trainees are expected to be able to climb poles, install transformers, and splice wires. How can a computer give them practice in those things?

Performance-oriented trainers will be anxious to give you delivery systems that will match your need. But the few who are more interested in pushing the "latest thing" can break you. So when you need to verify that a media decision is reasonable, review your objectives and make sure you can answer *yes* to each of these questions:

- Will the delivery system (combination of proposed media) give trainees practice in doing what the objectives say they should be able to do, and give them feedback when they do it?

- Is it the cheapest delivery system that will meet that goal?

- Is it readily available?

- Is it the alternative that will be least likely to break down?

- Can it be used in all of the places where instruction will be delivered (remote locations, field offices, and so on)?

- If live instructors are included in the delivery system, will they be readily available and properly trained?

KEY STEPS IN THE DEVELOPMENT OF INSTRUCTION DESIGNED TO ACCOMPLISH JOB-DERIVED OBJECTIVES

➤ **Before Initiating Training Development**

Verify the training need.

Decide on a course of action.

➤ **When Training Development Is Indicated**

Derive the objectives (expected outcomes).

Describe the training audience.

Draft skill hierarchies.

Review existing resources.

Determine the scope of instruction.

Draft skill checks.

Derive instructional content.

Select the delivery system (media mix).

Draft the instructional units.

Conduct tryouts.

Deliver the instruction.

Improve as required.

Draft the instructional units. Once the above steps have been completed, the developers will be ready to start drafting the instruction. Many developers will begin by drafting the end of the lesson first—the practice and feedback portion—and then add material to teach trainees whatever they need to know to get them ready for that practice. This helps them ensure that the critical practice component will always be included, and that irrelevant content will be excluded.

To get the job done quickly, the developers may need information from one or more of your people. Don't bristle at that. After all, you want them to produce a product that will fit your needs, and they have to get the information they need from somewhere. If they can't get it from manuals, or from their own heads, they will have to come to you. Deal with this the same way as you deal with your accountant: grumble about the questions you're asked, if you must, but provide access to the answers. Good developers know how to collect information in the shortest time possible. Be glad they haven't decided to sit in their offices inventing the information they need. That's what they'd have to do if you refused them access to information. You can imagine the risk you'd run in withholding needed information if that infomation were technical. (Imagine what the results would look like if you made your accountant invent the information he or she needs, just because you couldn't find the time to supply it.)

TYPICAL NON-TRAINING ACTIVITIES

➤ **Orientation sessions.** The purpose of these sessions usually is to acquaint new hires with the "lay of the land," company policies, and the location of the restrooms.

➤ **Information sessions.** The purpose of these sessions is to inform people of various developments: current events, new policies, coming products, and so on. These are "awareness" or "exposure" sessions that are unrelated to sessions designed to impart skill.

➤ **Team-building sessions.** The purpose of these sessions is to provide enjoyable activities (golf, baseball games, and so on) or stressful activities (such as river rafting or mountain climbing), through which managers can become better acquainted. The hope is that new channels of communication among them will be developed.

➤ **Motivation sessions.** These sessions are designed mainly to stimulate or generate enthusiasm for an activity or organization. (They might include rallies, song fests, storytelling, parties, and so on.)

➤ **Reward sessions.** Sometimes workers are sent to a course as a reward for accomplishments. Usually it is located in a desirable or exotic location. These courses may or may not have anything to do with the knowledge and skill needs of those attending.

Although these activities may have value, and although trainers are usually the ones assigned to organize them, they should not be looked upon as "training" sessions. And because they are not training sessions one should not expect the procedures described in this chapter to be applied to their preparation.

By the way, trainers may offer several non-training activities that seem very much like instruction. These are usually motivational sessions that look like instruction and are organized by trainers, so they often are mistakenly referred to as "training sessions." This is misleading, because the purpose of these sessions is not to help people develop skills. These non-training sessions can be important, but to refer to them as *training* may cause trainers to apply more technology than they need. (See page opposite for a description of typical non-training sessions.)

Conduct Tryout(s). All serious trainers will want to test instruction to make sure it works before they put it on line. That shouldn't surprise you. After all, manufacturers test products before they sell them, producers try out plays off Broadway to see if they "fly," and cooks often taste food before serving it. Just because instruction wasn't tested in the past doesn't mean it shouldn't have been.

Two kinds of testing are common. One involves testing bits and pieces of the course during the development itself, somewhat like the cook who keeps tasting along the way to the completed meal. The other involves testing of the complete product.

Ideally, tryouts and revisions continue until only cosmetic changes remain. The real world seldom allows such luxury, of course, because those for whom the instruction is being developed are usually in a great hurry to get it. In such cases the developers will ask the client to consider the first on-line offering as a dress rehearsal. It's best, therefore, not to insist that large quantities of materials be printed or duplicated until there is reason to believe that no further major changes will be needed.

Deliver the instruction. When the instruction has been nailed together, it is ready for use. With the instructional tools available today, it is possible to tailor instruction to the needs of the individual trainee so that each will have to study and practice only those components not yet mastered. Application of these tools leads to enormous savings of trainee time as well as of trainee motivation. All of the instructional time is productive, because no one is required to wait around while the slower ones catch up.

The secret to adjusting instruction to suit the individual is in the way the materials are developed, and in the rules by which the instruction is delivered. A common delivery rule is this:

Trainees study and practice until they can demonstrate the achievement of an objective; then they move ahead to the next objective.

With this rule in place it is possible to break the lockstep by which much instruction is dispensed, even when some of the learning is done in a group setting and involves group activities.

HOW LONG DOES ALL THIS TAKE?

"Holy smoke," you might be thinking, "training development must take forever." Not true. Sometimes it may seem like that, but developers who know their craft can get the job done in a lot less time than "forever." Besides, development projects are like salamis—some are shorter than others. The actual development time will depend on variables, such as:

• The subject matter

• Access to performance information and standards

- Thoroughness of the analysis (The more thorough the analysis, the shorter the development time.)
- The skill of the developers
- The difficulty in preparing materials for the media chosen

WHAT IF LEAD TIME IS SHORT?

There is another way to think about the entire process when lead time is short, as it usually is. Instead of asking, "How long will it take to develop my course?" you might consider asking,

"What can you do for me with the lead time I've got?"

After all, you want your people doing what they need to be doing in the least possible time. When lead time is short you may be able to do without the trappings of a formal course, while still getting most or all of what you need to develop the desired performances. This is true because no matter how short the lead time, trainers can provide useful services to help solve your problem. How do they do that? It's called *frameworking*—so named because the procedure fills in the performance framework by adding as many critical pieces as time will allow.

Think of the short lead time situation as a downpour. You're out in the woods, it's raining hard, and you want to get out of it. So what would you do if you only had time to do *one* thing? You'd probably try to get a roof or some equivalent over your head. That would be a great help all by itself, *even if you had no time to do anything else.* If you had time to do still one more thing, you might make a fire to get warm. If you had time to do one more thing, you might get out of your wet clothes and into some dry ones. That would probably be the next most useful thing you could do, even if you had no time to do anything else. And so on. Each thing you would select to do would be the thing that would give you the next most additional benefit.

Trainers can do that, too. No matter how short the lead time, they can do at least one thing that will be *immediately useful* to you. For example, if they have only two days for training development, the most useful thing they can do is to verify whether training is a valid solution, and to verify which solutions will have the greatest impact on the problem.

If the trainers have time to do one more thing, a task analysis would be the most useful action. These analyses can be turned into checklists in a matter of minutes, and the checklists can be given immediately to the instructors (trained or not) and to the trainees, to show trainees and instructors alike what competent performers do. With just that amount of guidance, trainees usually can tell which steps they already know how to complete and which they need to learn and practice. Instructors can use the checklists as a guide to make sure they deal with each of the items essential to competent performance.

If there is time to do one more thing, trainers can derive the objectives of the instruction and then draft skill checks by which instructional success can be measured. These items are also immediately useful, because they clearly describe the important outcomes of the instruction (that is, they make the goal posts visible) and suggest ways to measure whether those outcomes have been accomplished.

If more time is available, then the trainers can develop instructional lessons or units. In any case, however, development wouldn't begin until the previous steps have been completed. The fact that the results of these steps can be made useful immediately to you is frosting on the cake.

You can see, though, that if you ask the question, "How long will it take to develop this course?" you will get a far different answer than if you ask, "What can you do for me within the lead time I've got (whether it's a day or a year)?"

In order of payoff, the sequence in which items should be added to the development framework is as follows. Use this as a checklist to make sure the trainers make the best use of available time and to make sure you are allowed to put the results of each activity into practice as soon as it is completed.

1. Verify the need for instruction (for example, through performance analysis).

2. Describe the key components (steps, decisions, and so on) of competent performance (for example, through task and goal analyses).

3. Translate analysis results into checklists or other descriptions of competence.

4. Draft descriptions of intended outcomes (results and accomplishments); in other words, draft objectives.

5. Draft instruments through which to measure accomplishment of the objectives (that is, skill checks).

6. Draft a description of the intended trainee audience (target population description).

7. Collect existing pieces of instruction from manuals, texts, films, videos, and so on, that appear relevant to teaching one or more objectives, and key them to the pertinent objectives.

8. Draft an instructional unit to teach the one concept or skill that is most crucial to competent performance and that currently is lacking for most target trainees.

9. Draft an instructional unit to teach the next most critical concept or skill needed by the greatest number of trainees.

10. Repeat step 9 until all instruction is developed, or until time runs out.

(A reviewer of one of the tryouts of this book made this comment about the preceding checklist: "If trainers always did this, training and performance costs would plummet, and the impact on performance nationwide would be heard as far away as Tokyo.")

UNRULY RULES OF THUMB

Some trainers operate on a rule of thumb that says, "It takes 100 hours to develop one hour of instruction." For others, the magic number is 300 hours, or 40 or 60 hours. Having read the section above, you can see the problem with this kind of thinking. Development time is influenced by several variables, and to spout a "rule of thumb" here suggests that training development follows a fixed ritual that requires a fixed amount of time. Of course, you will need an estimate of what a development project will cost. But that estimate should be based on the nature of the project, rather than on a shaky rule of thumb. So, *avoid asking how long it will take to develop your instruction until you know for sure that instruction will help, and until the objectives of that instruction have been drafted.*

AN EXAMPLE

Here's an example that illustrates the sort of flexibility you can expect from professional trainers:

Some managers at a large utility company decided they wanted each worker in the reprographic department (duplicating equipment) to be able to perform several jobs. Having made that decision, they might then have ordered 50 courses to be developed, one to teach operation of each of the 50 duplicating machines (printing presses, lithography, copiers, photographic equipment, and so on). The cost of that option would have been substantial.

Instead, the managers elected to teach each key person how to perform a task analysis on his or her own machine. Time required for this training: two days. Next, the workers themselves carried out a complete task analysis with the assistance and coaching of two professional analysts. Time for analysis of 50 jobs: two weeks. Each task analysis was then converted into a checklist of steps. Time required: three days, plus two days for review and corrections.

Once those steps had been completed, small booklets were prepared to serve as guidance for practice and testing. (Guess who printed the booklets?) The booklets included a checklist for each task performed on a single machine and a few sentences of instruction for whoever was going to set up a skill check. This material was placed on facing pages: instructions to the tester on the left, the checklist of task steps on the right.

The skilled operators used these booklets to train others as time became available. Because everyone was involved in the project, there were no secrets and therefore no problem with buy-in. Project completion time was short, no classrooms were required, and all of the training was done by the operators themselves (with guidance by professional trainers). Smooth!

Note: This example should not be taken to mean that all training can, or should, be carried out in the workplace. When possible, however, it can provide a less expensive option than the formal classroom.

NEXT?

You're ready to call the trainers for services.

6

How to Deal with Trainers

Suppose you walked into a tailor shop and heard the following conversation between the tailor and a customer:

Customer: I'd like you to tailor me a suit of some fine material, and I'd like it to fit me to a T.

Tailor: Excellent. Let me just take your measurements.

Customer: Wait a minute. I haven't got time for that sort of thing. Look. *You're* the tailor. Go into your back room and make me a suit, and don't bother me while you're doing it!

Would you think it a little odd that the customer didn't insist on selecting the cloth? Or being measured for size? Or being asked what he or she intended to do in the suit?

You may think this scenario rather bizarre and unlikely, and perhaps it would be—in the tailoring business. After all, people who want a tailored suit tend to know the rules of the game. But it's the sort of thing that some managers do to trainers all the time. They say to a trainer, "I want a course," or "I need to have my people trained in _____ ," and then insist that the trainers run off to their back rooms and develop the product in question, without ever "taking measurements" and without ever analyzing the need so that a

THE FULL-SERVICE TRAINING &
PERFORMANCE SERVICES DEPARTMENT

Here is a list of some of the services that might be offered by a performance-oriented full-service department.

Needs analyses

A review of organizational plans to identify needs for training and non-training services.

Performance analyses

On-site review to identify causes of discrepancies between actual and desired performance, with recommendations for solutions.

Feedback review

An on-site review to ensure that all tasks include sources of feedback to the performers.

Consequence review

An on-site review intended to ensure that the consequences for desired performance are favorable to the performer.

Task analyses

On-site analyses intended to generate descriptions of actual and/or exemplary performance.

Goal analyses

A technique intended to assist managers in developing usable definitions of abstract intents.

Organizational analyses

A review of the organizational structure within and around a job, intended to determine whether the organizational structure facilitates or impedes peak performance.

Documentation

Manuals, and so on, designed to be used to facilitate job performance.

Job/performance aids

Design and development of items that will prompt desired performance.

Performance management systems

Development of mechanisms and procedures intended to ensure a supportive environment.

Workplace review

On-site review intended to identify obstacles caused by awkward workplace design.

Orientation sessions

Sessions that allow people to become familiar with target concepts and information.

Training sessions

Sessions intended to teach people what they do not currently know but need to know.

Coaching instruction

Training sessions for non-trainers who will be expected to conduct on-the-job training.

solution can be tailored to fit. When the trainers express the desire to look at the environment in which the skills will be used, and to learn something about those people who will be trained, they are often told, "Look. You're the trainer. So go develop my course and don't bother me or my people while you're doing it."

But if managers wouldn't tolerate tailors who don't take their measurements, why would they tolerate trainers who don't insist on creating solutions that will fill their needs? If you went to your physician to ask for help, wouldn't you insist on being examined, and insist on being allowed to describe your symptoms, before a remedy was prescribed? Sure, you're a busy person. And of course you don't want outsiders clogging your operation. But if you call the trainers because you've got a problem, wouldn't you want to get your money's worth?

Trainers skilled in their craft can, and are eager to, do just that. They know how to train, of course, and they know how to do it efficiently. But they also know how to help you to avoid training when a cheaper and faster remedy will get the results you want. And when your people truly need training, trainers can get the job done in ways that will keep your people away from their jobs for the shortest time possible.

With that said, it's time to describe a strategy for getting the services you need from your trainers. Here's how to do it.

BEFORE YOU ASK FOR SERVICES

Get a list. If you haven't already done so, ask your trainers for a list of the services they provide. Almost every training department offers at least some non-training services, and each department will offer a different blend than others— all the more reason to find out what they have in stock. (See page opposite for a partial list of possible services.) Once you know what is available in the "training store," you will be better able to decide when to call that store for help. After all, if training were their only service, as far as you knew, you would be unlikely to call on them for help when you needed something else.

So find out about the main offerings of the training department. If the staff hands you a catalog of their current courses, thank them and then ask them again for a list of their other services. If they don't have one already available, suggest that they may be more likely to sell their wares if they would let others know what those wares are. (A few training directors may balk at providing a list of services. Their viewpoint may be that managers should just bring their problems to the trainers so that they and the managers can sort them out together. Although this position may have merit, it is still reasonable for you to want to know what you can get in the training store.)

Do a little sleuthing. Suppose you call your TV repair shop because your television set has stopped working. So old Harold comes out, takes a quick look, plugs the power cord back into the outlet, and hands you a bill for the service call. You'd feel a little silly calling in a professional to do something you could have done for yourself. You'd also feel a little poorer. It's like that with human performance, too. Sometimes we call in the pros when we can get the performance we want by doing the equivalent of plugging in the power cord. For example, we might let people know precisely what is expected of them, or we might remove obstacles that are interfering with accomplishment.

So, before you call the trainers, do a little performance analysis, if for no other reason than to avoid being embarrassed. After all, you don't want to have the trainers come in only to find that the power cord has been kicked out of the socket. Besides, you may be able to solve the problem by yourself.

ASKING FOR TRAINING SERVICES

When you decide to ask for services, you're going to have to talk either with the training manager or with one or more of the training staff. That isn't any different from talking with someone else, except for one thing. Unless you know for a fact that your people cannot now do what you want them to do, don't go to the training staff with a request for training. Take this as your rule of thumb: *Never ask a trainer for training!*

Ask for skills, ask for assistance with performance problems, ask for objectives to be derived, ask for job aids, manuals, feedback systems, for help with task or goal analyses, or for any other service. But don't ask for training. Why? If the training department is staffed by subject matter experts who don't know much about the training craft, and if you ask for training, you may get it, even if you don't need it. And that could cost you dearly. If it's staffed by expert trainers, they may have to find tactful ways to convince you to take another look at the situation. And that could take time.

1. Describe the problem or ask for outcomes. Tell the trainers what your people need to be able to do that they cannot now do. Describe the machines they need to be able to operate, the tasks they need to be able to perform, the accomplishments they need to be able to achieve. Here are some examples of the approaches you might use:

- "My order takers don't know how to use the new software they will be getting next month."

- "My sales staff need to convert features of the new line into customer benefits."

- "I have six people who need to be able to use the DDD Spreadsheet program by next Friday."

COMPARING TWO APPROACHES TO TRAINING

This chart highlights the main distinctions between the features of a systematically designed performance-based course and a conventional content-based course.

Performance-Based Course

1. Objectives are derived from analysis of real world needs and describe intended results.

2. Content of the instruction is derived from the objectives to be accomplished.

3. Trainees study only what they do not yet know.

4. Each trainee is given an opportunity to practice each objective.

5. Instruction includes only what is needed to accomplish the objectives.

6. The primary instructor role is that of coaching.

7. Tests (skill checks) are used for diagnosing difficulties, confirming mastery, and as opportunities to make trainees feel good about their progress.

8. Trainees study and practice until they have reached mastery of the objectives.

9. On reaching mastery, trainees receive a Certificate of Achievement.

Content-Based Course

1. Objectives typically are absent or used to describe the content to be covered.

2. Content of the instruction is usually determined by a subject matter specialist.

3. All trainees study the same content.

4. Trainees are given few opportunities to practice the entire objective.

5. Instruction may include content irrelevant to the need.

6. The primary instructor role is that of presenting.

7. When used at all, tests are used mainly as a basis for grading; that is, as a basis for determining how well each student performed in comparison with other course attendees.

8. Trainees study until the fixed course time has ended.

9. At course completion, trainees receive a Certificate of Attendance.

- "We're rolling out a new product in three months and I need five of my people to be able to install and repair it."

- "My troubleshooters take too long to clear up some kinds of troubles, and I'm not sure whether they need training or something else."

- "My supervisors won't work as hard as I do."

- "We're changing our product mix and I'd like some help in re-aligning my organization."

- "I have three new hires I'd like to schedule for the next orientation session."

- "I need help in planning my subordinates' professional development."

2. Negotiate an agreement. Before you accept services, make sure you have an answer to the following questions:

- What services are we talking about?

- When will they be delivered?

- What will they cost?

- What will they be expected to accomplish?

- How will we measure results?

- What will I be expected to do, and when?

3. Verify that a performance-based approach will be used. Find out what kind of training approach the trainers intend to use. Because it can make so much difference in how well the instruction works and in how much it will cost, you will want to make sure that a performance-based (or outcome-oriented) approach is used, not only for the development of the instruction, but for its delivery as well. Pull out the following list of questions and tell the trainers you are going to want a *yes* answer to each one.

_____ Will the instruction be designed to accomplish pre-specified objectives?

_____ Will the objectives be derived from the job?

_____ Will there be skill checks with which the success of the instruction can be assessed?

_____ Will those skill checks match the objectives—that is, will they ask the trainees to do whatever it is the objectives require them to do?

_____ During the instruction, will trainees be given an opportunity to practice each of the skills described in the objectives?

_____ Will each trainee be required to study and practice only those skills that he or she is not yet competent in?

_____ Will each trainee be given enough practice to allow development of confidence in his or her ability to perform?

These same questions should be asked about courses already on the trainers' shelf. If the trainers are still using a content-oriented approach to training, encourage them to bring these courses up to a state-of-the-art approach, or try to buy your training from someone else. (See page 100 for a comparison of these two training approaches.)

4. Assist in the derivation of the objectives. To derive the objectives of the training, someone will need to complete a task analysis so that everyone will be able to see the elements of what competent performers do when they do it. Good analysts can accomplish this step without intruding on your operation. They may have to watch competent performers at work, but they will know how to do that without being intrusive. Expect the analysts to be the soul of tact and discretion. If the training department sends you someone who acts even remotely like a bull in a china shop, throw the bum out and demand a more tactful person. You shouldn't have to put up with anyone who doesn't know the craft.

It is likely that a few goal analyses will have to be completed along the way. If they're indicated, you should make sure they get done. Don't forget: the degree to which you speak in abstractions is the degree to which you abdicate control to someone else to decide what you mean.

5. Sign off on the draft outcomes. Insist on signing off on the proposed objectives of the instruction before allowing development to begin. This will be your opportunity to make sure that you won't be paying for more instruction than you need. Those objectives will also serve as your "contract" with the trainers whose job it will be to prepare people to perform according to the objectives.

If you are thinking about using a course that is already being offered, either by your trainers or by vendors, ask for a copy of the course objectives. Compare that list against your own needs. If there is a match, the course probably will be useful to you. If there is little overlap between your own objectives and those of the existing course you are considering, reject it. Never mind what the course is called, reject it. It would only be a waste of your resources. And, of course, if there aren't any objectives to look at, don't waste your time with it.

6. Agree on the training location. There are a number of places where the training might be delivered, including:

In a classroom • On the job • At a place close to the job

At home or in one's car (self-study)

In a combination of locations

You will want to negotiate a training location that will:

a. Remove your people from their work stations for the shortest time possible.

b. Ensure that they will have ample opportunity to practice the objectives to be achieved.

c. Be least distracting to the trainees.

It is often less expensive and less time-consuming to arrange for the training to be done on the job or at some location near the job, such as in a room nearby. But don't choose that option unless you can provide a distraction-free environment for the training. A distracting learning environment will lead to less effective training that takes longer to complete. Managers who expect people to work and learn at the same time are fooling themselves. If there is something serious to be learned, it needs to be studied in a distraction-free environment. If that means a location away from the workplace, that's the option you should choose. Above all, select an option that will allow trainees to get practice in what they are learning.

7. Provide access. During the development of training, the developers will need two things from you.

Access to information: If the developers are not experts in the subject matter that will be the target of the instruction, they will need access to that information. Make one or more competent performers available to them. If they know their jobs, the developers will know how to get the information they need in the least amount of time.

Access to target trainees: Ultimately, the developers will want to test the instruction on one or more of the people for whom it is intended. Cooperate to the best of your ability. Tryout is important to the success of the training, and you will be doing yourself a favor by smoothing the way. If it is completely impossible to arrange for even a small tryout of the instruction, demand that the first on-line course offering be considered a try-out. Don't let the trainers print more materials than will be needed for that first run-through; that way, you won't have to throw away materials that are made obsolete by the opportunities for improvement revealed by the tryout.

8. Prepare your trainees. Before you let your people head for the training, get them ready. Conduct a short goal-setting meeting during which you discuss the objectives of the instruction and the way in which the new skills will fit into the overall functioning of your organizational unit.

Some training departments offer a support workshop for supervisors of workers scheduled to attend training in the near future. During this short workshop, supervisors are given an overview of the training objectives and methodology that will be used. If your organization offers such a service, it would be well worth the time to attend.

Preparing your trainees for the training they will receive is an important step in making it successful. It will tell the trainees that you consider the training to be an important activity and that you are interested in having them learn what the training has been designed to teach. It will also tell them that you expect them to be able to apply the learned skills when the training has been completed. (If any of these things is not true, you shouldn't be sending them to training in the first place.)

9. Stay clear of the training. While the training is going on, stay clear. You are an authority figure whose very presence will interfere with your people's ability to learn. Don't kid yourself into thinking that you are "one of the boys," whose presence won't be noticed. Don't distract them.

I recall a workshop during which two young men from a glass company expressed a great deal of enthusiasm for the skills being taught. This was the first time their organization had sent them to training away from home, and they were bursting with pride, for themselves as well as for their company. Then one day, their boss managed to slip into the classroom without being seen, and he berated his trainees in front of everyone else for not wearing their ties. Because of the informal workshop atmosphere, nobody was wearing a tie, but that didn't stop the boss. As a result of this humiliating treatment, these two talented young men not only left the workshop, they quit their jobs and went to work for a competitor.

> **Warning:** Sometimes managers call the trainers to ask, "How're my people doing?" expecting that the trainer will provide an evaluation of the abilities and potential of the trainees. This is not a trainer's responsibility, and you shouldn't expect a knowledgeable trainer to respond with anything more than a polite "They're doing fine." Or, a manager may be tempted to ask a trainer to write an evaluation of the trainees. Again, such a request is out of line. Trainers teach each other how to refuse these requests tactfully.

What's so bad about asking a trainer to evaluate your people for you? For one thing, that's your job. For another, trainers don't necessarily know how to do that. But the main reason is that it can have a devastating effect on the trainees. People who are learning are vulnerable. They are exposing their ignorance—that's why they're in training—and they are easily thrown off balance. If they know that their every move will be evaluated, whether related to the skills they are learning or not, they may simply freeze up and close themselves to the instruction. How would you feel if every one of your practice golf swings was graded, and if you knew that those grades would go directly to your boss? How would you feel if you thought that the trainers were feeding information to your boss about your deportment, and your attitude, and about their judgment of your future potential?

WHEN YOU NEED A NON-TRAINING SERVICE

If you need one or more other remedies to improve performance rather than training (remedies such as job aids, documentation, feedback system, or an incentive or reward system), here's what to do.

1. Meet with the training staff. Discuss the proposed remedies with one of the performance analysts in the training department. Try to reach an agreement on who will do what to get the problem solved. In the following example, a manager discusses a non-training solution with a performance analyst. An analysis has shown that a job aid will be useful.

Manager: I agree that a well-prepared checklist will give my people instant access to the information they need to answer customer questions that are phoned in. How long will it take you to develop it?

*Performance
Analyst:*   We can have a draft for your approval by
next Tuesday. We'll need to get information
from one or more of your people, to make
sure we include all of the items in the right
order. Who can we talk to?

Manager: Talk to Sam Nozitall. He's the most experienced hand, and will have the information
you need. I'll call him in so that we can set
up a schedule.

*Performance
Analyst:*   Good. You'll have the draft by next Tuesday.

2. Review the draft of the proposed remedy. Check the
draft when it arrives from the training staff. Make sure it
addresses the problem that you need to solve. If the item
involves print, such as a checklist, give the draft to one of
your less experienced people to review. You might say
something like, "Here's a draft of the checklist I told you
about. I'd appreciate your reviewing it to see if you think it
will be easy enough to use. In particular, I'd like you to try
it out, to make sure the size of the binder will be the most
practical. Your suggestions will be welcome."

If the service involves feedback, or a change in the way
performance consequences (rewards) will be handled, make
sure the consequences suggested by the analysts will be
within your control to use and favorably viewed by those
who receive them.

3. Prepare your people. Regardless of the intervention being developed, it will smooth the way if you inform people
of the coming change. If appropriate, get them involved in
planning for the implementation.

4. Implement the remedy. Often a remedy can be implemented with no more fanfare than that of introducing or passing along the items in question. For example, you might just say, "Charlie, here is the checklist we discussed. Let me know how well it works," or "Erica, here is the user manual we had developed for the numerical controllers. When you use it, please mark any problems you find with it."

When the remedy involves more than just job aids, though, such as a change in policy or a change in organizational structure, applying the remedy successfully needs somewhat more attention. Even though you may have prepared your people for the change, do something when the change actually happens to convince them of your interest in successful application. A good way to do this is to be personally involved at the beginning. Tell people again how interested you are in making this solution work, and ask for their feedback.

5. Monitor the results. Be sure to monitor the situation shortly after the solution has been put on line. Check that it is working the way it is supposed to work. If it isn't, call the analyst back in to see what adjustments might be needed.

Trainers skilled in their craft are prepared to solve problems rather than just train. The secret to getting the kind of services that will lead to peak performance from your staff is to make sure those problems are well defined before asking for services. If you don't have the time to do it, get an analyst to do it. But do it.

6. Keep the trainers informed. Who are the people that you routinely keep informed of your management plans? Does that list include the trainers? If it doesn't, add them to the list. The more they know about your plans, the better able they will be to help you accomplish those plans. For example, when you learn that a new product will be introduced in a few months' time, inform the trainers now rather than the day before you want the training. Better yet, invite them to your planning meetings. That way they will be able to plan along with you and will be more likely to have the resources you need, when you need them.

WHERE WE'RE HEADED

Your trainees will soon be returning from the training. Will you be ready for them? Will you know how to get your money's worth from your training investment? The next chapter will show you how.

7

How to Get Your Money's Worth

Now that your trainees will be returning from training with their new skills, it would be easy to conclude that the job is done. You've helped specify exactly what it is that your people need to be able to do that they couldn't do, and the trainers have prepared and delivered instruction that guarantees those skills to be in place.

What more is there to do?

Remember the expression "Use it or lose it"? Well, if those skills are to be available when they are needed, and if they are to improve over time, it will be because of what you do when your trainees return. It's your turn to take action. After all, a contract isn't complete until both parties have fulfilled their obligations. So the ball is now in your court. Here's why.

As you already know, skill is not enough. As you learned in Chapter 1, successful job performance depends on four conditions: skill, self-confidence, the opportunity to perform, and a supportive environment. If the training was properly designed and executed, the trainers will have provided the first two of these conditions—the skills and the confidence to apply the skills.

But only you can supply the opportunity to perform, and the supportive environment to maintain the performance. So you have a critical role to play when the trainees return from training. To get your money's worth from training, then, here are the few things that you need to do to keep the new skills from leaking out under the door.

PREPARING FOR THE
RETURN OF YOUR TRAINEES

While the training is still in progress, review the objectives of the training and ask yourself these questions. When you can answer *yes* to each one, you will be ready for their return.

_____ 1. Will they know exactly what accomplishments they will be expected to produce?

_____ 2. Will they have the opportunity to exercise their new skills within a week or two after returning?

_____ 3. Will they have the tools, authority, place, and time to use the skills they just learned?

_____ 4. Has someone been assigned the job of checking that the new skills are being applied to your satisfaction?

_____ 5. Do you know how to respond favorably when people perform competently? That is, do you know what you will do or say to recognize instances of desired performance?

WHEN THEY RETURN TO THE JOB

Ask for a skill list. You already have a list of the objectives that the instruction was supposed to accomplish. Now that the training is over you will want to know what to expect each trainee can do that he or she couldn't do before. If the trainers don't provide you a list of the objectives accomplished by each trainee, or some other description of their demonstrated accomplishments, expect your trainees to bring it with them. This list will serve as a "window sticker," to identify what a person has accomplished. If you don't get such a list, ask for it. After all, there may be good reasons why trainees didn't accomplish all of the objectives; there may also be reasons why trainees accomplished more than was expected.

Help trainees apply new skills. Do what you can to make sure that the skills that have just been learned are used, preferably within a week or so of their being learned. Provide the necessary tools, authority, time, and space to do the things they just learned how to do. If you can't arrange for immediate opportunities for the skills to be used on the job, find some way to provide periodic practice off-line. Use it or lose it.

MAKING THE PERFORMANCE
EVEN BETTER

To make the learning stick you need to get the skills used. To make the performance improve, do these things.

Check for obstacles to performance. It's easy for glitches to crop up once in a while that get in the way of peak performance. And every once in a while someone needs to get out the "glitch-sniffer" and do an obstacle sweep. Fortunately, that isn't difficult. All you have to do is ask people if anything is interfering with their achieving the results you have prescribed. They will know, and they will be impressed that you should ask. So, ask—because there can be all sorts of obstacles, large and small, that can get in the way of performance. Many obstacles can be eliminated with the wave of a hand. Here are a few examples:

- The lack of information about job expectations

- Inadequate tools or supplies

- Parts bins in the wrong place

- Parts showing up late

- Work mounted at an awkward height

- Unattractive and oppressive work stations

- Poorly arranged computer monitors or other frequently used equipment

- Overloaded telephone systems

There are a thousand other such obstacles. (One of my otherwise brilliant colleagues tolerates a silly computer program that makes him hit the space bar *twice* between *each word* he types. Is that an unnecessary obstacle or what?) So, find the obstacles and get rid of them as best you can. Performance will improve, usually immediately. When you provide both opportunity to perform and a supportive environment, you can be assured that the skills you paid for will be there when they're needed.

Check for upside-down consequences. Because jobs and job conditions change when we're not looking, it's possible for the consequence structure (the structure of rewards and punishments) to get twisted out of shape. The results of doing a job right can become punishing, and the results of doing it wrong—or not at all—can become very attractive. So, it's worth finding out periodically whether the consequences support (encourage) desired performance or discourage it.

How can you check to make sure? The simple thing would be to call the training department and ask if they have a performance analyst who can conduct a consequence review. If so, the analyst will check to see what happens to workers when they do things right and when they do things wrong (by observing work and asking questions of workers). The analyst will then make confidential suggestions to you regarding positive actions you might take to remedy ineffective or topsy-turvy consequences.

If the training department doesn't provide such a service, you'll have to do it yourself. It isn't difficult to do. After preparing or locating lists of the tasks that workers are expected to perform, ask them to tell you what happens that they consider punishing (aversive). In other words, ask if there are consequences for desired performance that make their world dimmer or less pleasant. But unless you and your subordinates are completely open with one another, you will want the review conducted by a third party. The object of the review is to get an accurate picture of what happens to people when they perform to expectation and when they don't. You won't get an accurate picture if people feel that they have to hedge their responses in order to keep their jobs.

Check for feedback. It doesn't matter how many times a day a person repeats a performance; unless the person gets feedback on the quality of that performance, he or she cannot be expected to improve. Without feedback, there will be no reason for a person to change or adjust what he or she is doing. There will be no reason to take corrective action.

Lots of tasks have performance feedback built in. In these cases, workers can't help but find out whether their performance is or isn't okay. For example, if a part doesn't fit, the worker knows that something needs to be done differently. If the subassembly doesn't check out, the worker knows that an error needs correction. In these instances, no special attention to feedback is needed.

For lots of other tasks, though, information regarding the quality of the performance either doesn't exist or doesn't get back to the performer. Examples are endless: interviewers who never find out how well they're handling applicants; hotshot troubleshooters on the hot line who never find out that they may be insulting the customers; managers who never find out from their managers how well *they* are performing, until the day they get booted out the door; workers who aren't told that they are performing a task unsafely until they lose a finger or a hand; lawyers who never find out why they are being avoided.

It pays to ensure that there is adequate performance feedback for each of the job components. Fortunately, you don't have to do it all yourself. If your training and performance department provides the service, you can ask them to design any feedback systems you may need. Moreover, they can be called in periodically to do a feedback and consequence review, which is something like checking for safety hazards. Such a review is relatively simple to do and takes little time. It requires reviewing the desired performances and expected job accomplishments, and then checking to make sure that (a) there is feedback regarding the quality of the performances, and (b) the consequences for the desired performance and accomplishments are favorable rather than punishing.

Skilled analysts will be happy to work as your confidential assistant and will report their findings directly to you and to no one else. That will provide you with clues about how to improve performance even more.

Recognize desired performance. People tend to continue to do those things for which they receive recognition and reward. If they continue to do them, and receive feedback regarding the quality of their performance, their performance very likely will improve over time. It pays off, therefore, to catch people doing something right, and to *let them know* that you've noticed.

WRAPPING UP

The responsibility for getting people to perform on the job cannot be left to the trainers, because what *you* do contributes an important part of the performance equation. The best results are achieved when you view trainers as *partners in performance.* So, put them on your performance team. The results are well worth the effort.

8

How to Do It Yourself

When someone in your department needs training, you have two choices: have someone else do it, or do it yourself. You already know what to do when you are going to have someone else do it. But if there are times when you will have to do some of it yourself, you'll want to know how. As you've seen throughout this book, people don't become competent trainers just because they go to school or because they happen to be good at what they do. And, the techniques applied at school aren't necessarily the way things are done when results matter.

Why would you want to do any training yourself? There may be several reasons. There may not be time to get someone else to do it. Or the job may be too small to farm out. Or you may be grooming someone to take your place so you can be promoted to bigger and better things. Whatever the reason you find yourself in the trainer's role, there are some things you need to know to help you succeed. Knowing them will make your training smoother and shorter. These techniques will send your trainees away ready to apply their new skills and eager to learn more.

To get you there, we'll consider a few key facts about how learning happens, and then I'll offer a checklist of steps that will help you make sure you are applying the main learning principles to your instruction.

TIPS ABOUT LEARNERS

Let's begin by thinking about the target of the instruction, the trainee. The more you know about trainees, the better you can tailor your instruction to their needs. All human learners have several things in common.

- Everyone comes to the learning situation with a lifetime of experience, regardless of age.

- The lifetime experiences of each learner are different from those of others.

- Lifetime experiences include the ability to perform many skills.

- Lifetime experience also includes misconceptions, biases, prejudices, and preferences. In other words, some of what people think they know is actually wrong.

- People who are consciously trying to learn something new are vulnerable.

- All learners tend to avoid the things that cause them pain or embarrassment. If an instructor causes them to be embarrassed, they will begin to avoid learning, and they will learn to avoid that instructor.

- All learners feel good about themselves when their learning is recognized or when something good happens to them as a result of their learning progress and successes.

What this means is that people come to the learning situation already knowing many things, some of which aren't true. They come with biases and prejudices, some of which will interfere with learning. People about to learn how to do things they haven't done before are vulnerable; they are concerned about doing well, and they avoid situations in which they believe they will be laughed at, belittled, humiliated, or embarrassed.

LEARNING PRINCIPLES

Relax. This isn't going to turn into a lecture on the theory of learning. Even if you knew everything there is to know about learning theory, it wouldn't necessarily make your instruction more successful. (Lots of poor instructors are well versed in learning theory.) But out of the entire mountain of learning lore there are a few principles that may help you understand why the checklist at the end of this chapter includes the items it does.

Attention

As the farmer said when he whacked his mule with a two-by-four, "First you've got to get their attention." That's true with learners, too. Before you begin to teach them something, you've got to turn their attention in the direction of the learning. Not only do you need to attract their attention to the fact that they are being taught something, you need to make sure they attend to the critical features of the item to be learned. Just exposing people to information isn't good enough. Telling isn't the same as teaching. Whether you are explaining or demonstrating something, you must call attention to the key components of the item to be learned.

For example, suppose you are demonstrating the correct

way to conduct a meeting. To call attention to an important point, you might find yourself saying, "The first critical step is the agenda. Unless you have an agenda that is written down, you aren't ready to call a meeting, no matter how important the topic. So the best way to decide if you're ready to call the meeting is to check your agenda. If you don't have one, you're not ready."

Another way to call attention to the important features of what you are teaching is to get the trainee to respond to those features. There are two ways to do this. You might ask a question, or you might ask the trainee to perform. My shooting instructor repeatedly asked, "What are you supposed to do with your eyes when you squeeze the trigger?" and I was supposed to respond, "Keep them both open." You might find yourself asking, "What must you do before calling a meeting?" and expecting the trainee to reply, "Have a written agenda."

Motivation

Just because you may be highly interested in a topic, that's no reason for anyone else to be interested in it. That may be a little hard to swallow, your being a manager and all, but you have to recognize this fact. People do those things they are interested in doing—and those things that are worth *their* while to do. When motivation principles are distilled to plain language, it comes down to this: before you start training, make sure your trainees know the answer to the question, "What's in it for me?" Trainers call this the WIIFM factor, and it is critical.

Suppose I tell you that it is important for you to memorize the Morse code because it would make me feel very good. Does that make you want to run out and buy a telegraph key? I doubt it. Suppose, on the other hand, I told you that learning Morse code may qualify you for promotion.

Never mind whether that's true. The point is that in the first instance I told you what's in it for me, and in the second instance I told you what's in it for you.

So, no matter what you are teaching, make sure the trainees know how it will matter to *them* to learn what you are teaching. Here are some examples:

- "The more service calls you make in a day, the more money you'll make. I'm going to teach you a trouble-shooting procedure that will help you find troubles so fast you'll double the number of service calls."

- "If you don't complete these forms right the first time, they'll be sent back to you to fix. That will take you more time."

- "If you learn how to acknowledge good performance, you'll be able to keep more of your good workers, and everyone will want to work harder for you."

Notice that in all of these examples the emphasis on "you."

Modeling

Most of what people learn is learned through imitation. We see someone do something, and we tend to do it that way ourselves. Because there is such a strong tendency to do it the way we've seen it done, it is important that you model the desired performance. In other words, make sure you do it the way you want others to do it. People who find themselves saying, "Don't do as I do, do as I say," are fooling themselves. People see, people do. Here are the key modeling principles, along with the implication for instruction:

Principle: Observers learn by watching and imitating others; they tend to behave as they have seen others behave.

Implication: Behave as you want others to behave.

✦

Principle: Observers will be more likely to imitate a model who has prestige in the eyes of the observer.

Implication: Have the desired performance demonstrated by someone your trainees respect—another manager or a local hero. If you have prestige in the eyes of your trainees, as you probably do, it's doubly important to practice what you teach.

◆

Principle: Observers will be more likely to imitate modeled performance when they observe the model being rewarded for that performance.

Implication: Make sure that when people perform as you expect them to, they are occasionally rewarded for that performance. This will increase the probability that others will perform that way, too.

Modeling principles operate whether we like it or not. The best way to avoid violating those principles is simply to perform the way you want others to perform. In other words, do unto others.

Retention

There are two things to think about here. One of them is the process of getting information and skills into the learner, and the other is the process of getting performance out of the learner. Unless learners can recall what they have learned, they can't apply what they have learned.

This is an important consideration, because it is too easy to teach people things in ways that will inhibit remembering. It is too easy to get information and skills into a person, without putting hooks on it so that it can be pulled out again (that is, remembered). Fortunately, it isn't difficult to train in a way that will maximize the likelihood that the trainees will remember what they were taught. Here are some guides.

Timing: Plan for trainees to learn skills just before using those skills. You can see the folly of trying to teach an army private to be a general. Even if that private ultimately gets promoted to general, the chance that he or she will remember much about generaling is pretty slim. The same is true for most skills. If you teach something today that won't be used for a year, there isn't much point in bothering with the teaching. Save your time for something else.

I know, it isn't always possible to use a "just-in-time" approach to instruction. But the principles of learning don't bend for organizational convenience. Teaching it now, when it won't be used until much later, is bad practice if you want the skills available when they are needed.

Practice and feedback: If you want people to remember what you are teaching them, then make sure they practice it. Make sure they practice until they can do it right, and make sure they find out how well they're performing. Provide feedback in a positive way that will let trainees know what they are doing right and wrong and at the same time will build, rather than damage, their self-confidence.

If you're teaching knowledge, have the trainees verbalize the information—to say it out loud. If you're teaching them anything else that happens mainly inside the head (that is, thinking skills, problem solving, discriminating, and so on), make them verbalize the practice. Get them to talk it through, out loud.

Relevant practice: Arrange for the practice to occur under the same, or similar, conditions under which the performance will be expected to occur on the job. People are more likely to perform on the job when they have practiced under job conditions. In this case, the job environment itself will provide cues that will trigger the desired performance.

Linking the new to the familiar: If you tie new information to things the trainees already know, they will be more likely to remember it. Use analogies when possible, and move from the big picture toward the details, rather than from the details toward the whole.

> **Example:** "Now that you've had a tour of the production line and have seen what happens to the product at each step along the way, we can focus in on the details of the liquid soldering operation that you will be handling."

Reinforcement: When people long for the "good old days," it's often because they remember the good things that happened to them and have forgotten the bad things. The same holds true for learning. If the things we learn lead to pleasant events (for example, a smile or a favorable word from the instructor), we'll be more likely to remember those things than if the learning leads to unpleasant results. For better retention, then, as well as improved self-confidence, make sure you recognize trainees' progress. Say something good about their new performance, for example. Show people how to correct their errors, of course, but don't insult or belittle while you are doing so. In other words, provide a supportive environment.

That's enough about learning principles. Here are some guides to help you with the instructing itself. There are three parts:

- Getting ready to instruct

- Instructing

- Checking the results.

GETTING READY TO INSTRUCT

Decide on the outcomes. Until you know what you want the instruction to accomplish, you won't be able to decide what to teach or how to teach it. In addition, you won't be able to give your trainees a clear picture of their learning target.

You already know how important it is to derive the objectives of the instruction before turning the process crank. This is even more important when you are going to be doing the training yourself, because a clear statement of the objectives of the training will often relieve you of the need to do much more. Often, trainees will be ready to start practicing as soon as they know what it is you want them to be able to do. Also, a clear statement of the purpose of the training will make it easier for everyone to focus on the task at hand. So, write down the intended outcomes of the session, and be prepared to hand a copy to the trainees when they arrive. (If you need a little guidance, read *Preparing Instructional Objectives,* listed under Useful Resources, on page 147.)

If this seems like more work than you want to do, get one of the trainers to help you to work out the outcomes you want to accomplish.

Prepare the skill checks. If it's worth teaching, it's worth finding out whether the teaching worked. To draft a skill check, you need only review an objective and then decide how you are going to ask the trainees to do what the objective requires.

Thus, if an objective says, "Be able to interview...," you will arrange to observe the trainee actually interviewing. It may be a simulated interview, but the trainees will be asked to do what it is the objective says they're supposed to do.

If you ask trainees to perform only a portion of what the objective calls for, you will have to make inferences about whether they can perform the entire objective. Is that risky? It depends on the consequence of an error. If doing it wrong doesn't lead to serious consequences, then the risk is small. If, on the other hand, the consequence of an error can be serious, then the risk is too great. I suspect you wouldn't be too comfortable if you learned that a pilot's flight skills were tested by a multiple-choice exam because it was too inconvenient to set up a flight test.

Collect the practice material. You know you aren't going to instruct unless you can arrange for your trainees to practice what you are teaching them. So collect the things you will need to make that practice happen. Maybe you'll need only a pad of paper and a pencil. Maybe you'll need some tools or instruments. Whatever you need, collect it.

Locate a distraction-free environment. You and your trainees will become frustrated if you are constantly interrupted by telephones or by people wandering by. So find someplace away from the bustle of the job to do the instructing.

INSTRUCTING

Provide objectives. After setting them at ease, give the trainees the objectives of the session and explain the objectives, if necessary.

Provide the WIIFMs. *WIIFM* stands for "What's in it for me?" Explain how the intended instruction fits into the big picture, and how it will benefit *them* to learn what you are about to teach.

Explain and demonstrate the skills to be learned. Showing is better than telling. So show trainees what they are supposed to do, and explain as you go along. Explain why it is important to accomplish the task in this way, when to do the task, when not to do it, how to avoid the common hazards, and how to know when they are finished doing it.

The purpose of the demonstrations and explanations is to get your trainees to the point where they are ready to practice. Your goal is to get them to start practicing as soon as possible.

Provide practice and feedback. As soon as you can, get out of the trainees' way and let them take over the demonstrating and explaining. Stand beside or behind them while they practice what they need to learn. This may be a little painful at first while you watch them make mistakes. But the longer you delay the practice, the longer the instruction will take.

Provide feedback as they practice, but focus on the positive. Call attention to the things they are doing right, and, unless they are doing something that is dangerous, ignore what they are doing wrong. If you call attention only to the wrong behavior, you are likely to get more of this behavior rather than less of it. By all means, show them how to correct incorrect performance, but be sure to smile every time they do something a little better than they did it the last time. (If you wait for perfect performance before you say something nice, you'll make the learning take longer.)

Tell your trainees that you want them to practice until they feel confident that next week they will be able to perform what they have learned—without supervision. Then arrange for the practice to happen.

Provide remedial help. If a performance does not yet meet your expectations, diagnose the problem and provide remedial help. There are two main reasons why people can't yet perform the way they should:

1. They may not understand it yet.

2. They may not have had enough practice.

If the person doesn't yet understand, find out which "piece" is missing, and explain and demonstrate it again. If the person needs more practice, provide the opportunity.

CHECK THE RESULTS

Assess the learning. To find out whether the instruction worked, ask trainees to demonstrate that they have achieved each objective. This will give them an opportunity to feel good about themselves, especially if you say or do something positive in response to good performance.

If you notice that one or more people are performing to expectation during the practice session, no separate skill check will be needed. Say something positive and move them to the next thing to be learned.

Check for self-confidence. Ask the trainees whether they feel confident enough in their skills to perform them next week without supervision. If self-confidence is low—regardless of how confident you feel about their skills—offer an opportunity for more practice.

Celebrate the results. When the trainees have learned to perform all of the objectives, celebrate their (and your) success. Do something nice for them, or with them. Take them to lunch, have a dinner (with spouses present), give a certificate of achievement, send a note to your boss extolling the newly skilled people—with a copy to the "extollees," of course—or give them a little time off. You should be able to find at least three dozen things you might do (that don't have anything to do with salary increases) to recognize accomplishment.

Provide opportunity and support. When your newly-trained people return to their jobs, be sure to provide the opportunity and the support they need to perform their best.

SUMMARY

When you are faced with a need to do some training yourself, you will be successful if you follow the steps outlined below.

GETTING READY TO INSTRUCT

1. Decide on the outcomes and draft the objectives.

2. Prepare the skill checks.

3. Collect the practice material.

4. Locate a distraction-free environment.

INSTRUCTING

1. Provide trainees with the objectives.

2. Explain the WIIFMs ("What's in it for me?").

3. Explain and demonstrate the things to be learned.

4. Provide practice and feedback.

5. Provide remedial help when needed.

CHECKING THE RESULTS

1. Assess the learning. (Ask trainees to perform as the objectives require.)

2. Assess trainees' self-confidence level, and offer additional practice if it is still too low.

3. Celebrate the results.

If you find yourself doing a lot of your own training, you may want to attend one of the short "train the trainer" workshops that may be offered by your training department. This should take no longer than a day or two, if it is tailored to your specific need. That instruction should expand on the steps just described and should give you some practice at coaching. If you need to train, then attending such a workshop will be time well spent.

9
Handy Checklists

Why People Don't Do What They're Expected to Do   136

The Primary Performance Tools   137

Performance Analysis Checklist   138

Performance Problem Solution Checklist   139

How to Complete a Goal Analysis   140

How to Obtain Training Services   141

How to Obtain Non-Training Services   141

How to Verify that a Performance-Based Approach
    Will Be Used   142

Frameworking (What to Do When Lead Time Is Short)   143

How to Get Full Value for Your Training Investment   144

How to Do the Instructing Yourself   145

WHY PEOPLE DON'T DO
WHAT THEY'RE EXPECTED TO DO

➤ They don't know how to do it.

➤ They don't know what's expected of them.

➤ They don't have the authority to do it.

➤ They don't get timely information about how well they're doing. (In other words, they don't get feedback.)

➤ Their information sources (documentation) are poorly designed, inaccessible, or nonexistent.

➤ They don't have job aids to cue correct performance.

➤ Their work stations provide obstacles to desired performance.

➤ The organizational structure makes performing difficult.

➤ They're punished or ignored for doing things right.

➤ They're rewarded for doing things wrong.

➤ Nobody ever notices whether they perform correctly or not.

THE PRIMARY PERFORMANCE TOOLS

➤ Information

➤ Documentation

➤ Feedback

➤ Job aids (performance aids)

➤ Workplace design

➤ Organizational structure

➤ Permission (authority) to perform

➤ Consequence management (rewards and punishments)

➤ Training

PERFORMANCE ANALYSIS CHECKLIST

1 **Whose performance is at issue?**

2 **What is the performance discrepancy?**
a. What is actually happening?
b. What should be happening?

3 **What is the approximate cost of the discrepancy?**
(What would happen if you ignored the problem?)

4 **Is the discrepancy a skill deficiency?**
(Are they unable to do it?)

5 **Yes...it *is* a skill deficiency:**
a. Can the job or task be simplified?
b. Are the tasks performed often?
c. Will other factors impede performance?

6 **No...it is *not* a skill deficiency:**
a. Are the performers being *punished* for doing it right?
b. Are the performers being *rewarded* for doing it wrong?
c. Are there no *consequences* at all to the performer for performing, either right or wrong?
d. Are there *obstacles* to performing as expected?

7 **List the causes of the discrepancy.**

8 **Describe solutions.**

9 **Estimate the cost of each solution.**

10 **Select the cost-effective solutions that can be implemented (those that are practical to implement).**

11 **Implement the solutions.**

PERFORMANCE PROBLEM SOLUTION CHECKLIST

➤ **PROBLEM**

➤ **SOLUTIONS**

They *can't* do it, and...

the skill is used often:
- Provide feedback.
- Simplify the task.

the skill is used rarely:
- Provide job aids to prompt desired performance.
- Simplify the job.
- Provide periodic practice.

(Training will be required if the above remedies are inadequate.)

They *can* do it, but...

doing it right leads to punishment:
- Remove the sources of punishment.

doing it wrong is more satisfying:
- Remove the rewards for incorrect performance.

nobody notices when they do it right:
- Apply consequences to the *performer* for doing it right.

there are obstacles to performing as desired:
- Remove the obstacles (or help people work around them).

HOW TO COMPLETE A GOAL ANALYSIS

1   Describe your goal (in terms of
outcomes rather than in terms of process).

2   Describe what someone would have to do
or say or accomplish, for you to be willing
to say the goal has been achieved.

3   Sort the list. Identify remaining fuzzies
(abstractions) and replace them with the
performances that represent their meaning.

4   Write a complete sentence describing
each of the performances on your
final list.

5   Test to make sure you have all of the
components that are of importance
to you.

HOW TO OBTAIN TRAINING SERVICES

➤ Before You Ask for Services:

1. Get a list of the services available.
2. Complete a brief performance analysis.

➤ When Asking for Training Services:

1. Describe the problems or ask for outcomes rather than for training.
2. Negotiate an agreement for services.
3. Verify that a performance-based approach will be used.
4. Assist in the derivation of the objectives of the instruction.
5. Insist on approving the draft objectives.
6. Agree on a training location.
7. Provide access to information and people.
8. Prepare your trainees before the training begins.
9. Stay clear of the training environment during training.

HOW TO OBTAIN NON-TRAINING SERVICES

1. Discuss the proposed remedies with a performance analyst.
2. Review and test the draft of the proposed remedy plan.
3. Prepare your people.
4. Implement the remedy.
5. Monitor the results.

HOW TO VERIFY THAT A PERFORMANCE-BASED APPROACH WILL BE USED

Ask the following questions of any instruction you are having developed, or that you are proposing to buy from vendors. A *yes* answer to each will ensure that the instruction will meet your needs in a state-of-the-art format.

_____ Will the instruction be designed to accomplish pre-specified objectives?

_____ Will the objectives be derived from the job or some other part of the real world?

_____ Will there be skill checks (criterion tests) with which the success of the instruction can be assessed?

_____ Will those skill checks match the objectives—that is, will they ask the trainees to do whatever it is the objectives require them to do?

_____ During the instruction, will trainees be given an opportunity to practice each of the skills described in the objectives?

_____ Will each trainee be required to study and practice only those skills that he or she is not yet competent in?

_____ Will each trainee be given enough practice to allow development of confidence in his or her ability to perform?

FRAMEWORKING (WHAT TO DO WHEN LEAD TIME IS SHORT)

What Is Frameworking?

Frameworking is a development structure that ensures that each completed activity will be of maximum usefulness, even if time prevents completion of further development steps. The process requires that you repeatedly answer the question, "If there is time for only one more activity, what would be the most useful activity?"

Frameworking Assumes:

1. It is a waste to engage in any instructional development until a need for instruction has been verified.

2. It is more productive to spend limited time making the components of desired performance visible than to create or polish instruction.

How Does Frameworking Work?

In the order shown, complete as many of these steps as time will allow, and put the results of each step into practice as soon as it is completed.

1. Verify the need for instruction (for example, through performance analysis).

2. Describe the key components (steps, decisions, and so on) of competent performance (for example, through task and goal analyses).

3. Translate analysis results into checklists or other descriptions of competence.

4. Draft descriptions of intended outcomes (results and accomplishments); in other words, draft objectives.

5. Draft instruments through which to measure accomplishment of the objectives (that is, skill checks).

6. Draft a description of the intended trainee audience (target population description).

7. Collect existing pieces of instruction from manuals, texts, films, videos, and so on, that appear relevant to teaching one or more objectives, and key them to the pertinent objectives. Make these available to instructors and trainees alike.

8. Draft, test, and revise an instructional unit to teach the one concept or skill that is most crucial to competent performance and that currently is lacking for most trainees.

9. Draft an instructional unit to teach the next most critical concept or skill needed by the greatest number of trainees.

10. Repeat step 9 until all instruction is developed, or until time runs out.

HOW TO GET FULL VALUE FOR YOUR TRAINING INVESTMENT

➤ Preparing for the Return of Your Trainees

Take the actions necessary to enable you to answer *yes* to these questions:

_____ Will trainees know exactly what they will be expected to accomplish in their jobs?

_____ Will they have the opportunity to exercise their new skills within a week or two after returning?

_____ Will they have the tools, authority, place, and time to use the skills they just learned?

_____ Has someone been assigned the job of checking that the new skills are being applied to your satisfaction?

_____ Do you know how to respond favorably when people perform competently? That is, do you know what you will do or say to recognize instances of desired performance?

➤ After Your People Return from Training

1. Ask for a skill list.
2. Arrange for the skills to be applied.

➤ To Improve Performance

1. Eliminate obstacles to performance.
2. Eliminate upside-down consequences.
3. Make sure performance is accompanied by feedback.
4. Recognize, or reward, desired performance.

HOW TO DO THE INSTRUCTING YOURSELF

➤ Getting Ready to Instruct

1. Decide on the outcomes, and draft the objectives.
2. Prepare the skill checks.
3. Collect the practice material.
4. Locate a distraction-free environment.

➤ Instructing

1. Provide trainees with the objectives.
2. Explain the WIIFMs ("What's in it for me?").
3. Explain and demonstrate the things to be learned.
4. Provide practice and feedback.
5. Provide remedial help when needed.

➤ Checking the Results

1. Assess the learning. (Ask trainees to perform as the objectives require.)
2. Assess trainees' self-confidence level, and offer additional practice if it is still too low.
3. Celebrate the results.

USEFUL RESOURCES

Mager, Robert F. *Preparing Instructional Objectives.* Revised second edition. Belmont, CA: Lake Publishing, 1984.

Mager, Robert F. *Goal Analysis.* Second edition. Belmont, CA: Lake Publishing, 1984.

Mager, Robert F., and Pipe, Peter. *Analyzing Performance Problems.* Second edition. Belmont, CA: Lake Publishing, 1984.

Mager, Robert F., and Pipe, Peter. *Performance Analysis Worksheets.* Atlanta, GA: Center for Effective Performance, 1979.

Mager, Robert F. *Making Instruction Work.* Second edition. Belmont, CA: Lake Publishing, 1988.

Pryor, Karen. *Don't Shoot the Dog.* New York: Bantam Books, 1984.

Rummler, Geary A., and Brache, Alan P. *Improving Performance: How to Manage the White Space on the Organization Chart.* San Francisco: Jossey-Bass, 1991.

Zemke, Ron, and Kramlinger, Thomas. *Figuring Things Out.* Menlo Park, CA: Addison-Wesley, 1982.

On the Walls
of Time

"I object!" screamed the defendant.

"You can't object," replied the judge, whacking another pistachio with his gavel. "The trial hasn't even started yet."

"But the jury...," stammered the accused.

"Yes, yes," soothed the judge. "I can see them quite clearly from here, you know."

"But there are *twenty-seven* of them!" wailed the trampled one.

"Oh?" queried the judge, peering over his wire-rimmed lenses. "Is there one missing or something?"

"No, no, no," said the frustrated one. "There are too *many* of them. And besides, *they're* the guilty ones. *They're* the ones who trampled all over my manuscript."

"Guilty, you say?" The judge narrowed his baggy eyes at the overstuffed jury box. "Yes, yes, I can see that. Plain as day, you know. Question is, what are they guilty of?"

"What are they guilty *of?*" pleaded the woeful accuser.

The judge's head swiveled toward the ceiling. "There must be an echo in here. I just said that."

"*I'll* tell you what they're guilty of," said the determined one, reaching into his evidence-filled briefcase. "Manuscript harassment, that's what!"

"Oh, goody," enthused the judge. "As soon as you're finished with the charge, I can pronounce sentence. I always like that part the best, you know." He whacked another pistachio.

"Then I'll begin," began the harassed one. "Look over there," he said, pointing a wavering finger. "There's David Cram."

"Oh, my," sighed the judge. "Back again, is he?"

"Yes," replied the wounded one. "He's the one who helped ensure the continuity and content of the early manuscript draft."

"He'll get his," whacked the judge. "And soon, too."

"And over there," continued the browbeaten one, jabbing a straightened finger at several of the guilty ones, "are the ones who verified the technical accuracy of the content. There's Bonnie Abney, Paul Whitmore, and Bill Deterline. This clump over here made suggestions regarding the appropriateness of the content and poked at the clarity of the wording—Al Wilson, Kay Newell, Dan Lyons, Seth Leibler, Kit Grimm, Galen Royer, and Carl Welte.

"Over in that corner is Susan Corliss. She combed the manuscript with the finest-toothed, multi-colored comb I've ever been combed with. And in that row over there are Linda Brooks, Ken Lichtenstein, Bill McKendree, and Bob Brooks."

"Is that the lot?" queried the judge. "I'm running out of pistachios."

"No, no. Over there is Lola Lollapalooza, masquerading as Eileen Mager. She's the one kept me going the day I ran into a problem I didn't know how to solve."

"Tsk, tsk," tsked the judge. "Any more?"

"Yes, your dubiousness. There's Ann Parkman, Carl Winkelbauer, Marianne Hoffman, and Brad Mager. They were involved in the title check, along with Dan Raymond over there. And finally, there are those who tested the draft cover designs, to make sure the brilliant content wasn't wrapped in the equivalent of a brown paper bag. They are

Al Wilson, Steve Marks, Lola Lollapalooza (alias Eileen Mager again), Ted Strang, and John Zilisch."

"Surely there can't be more," incredulated the judge.

"Only one. See that lady over there with the evil glint and the cute little horns? That's Ina Tabibian. She was the editorial cleaner-upper-final-fixer of all the little discrepancies and out-of-whacknesses that needed putting into whack. And that's the lot."

"Oh, goody," clapped the judge. "Now I get to instruct the jury."

"But it's the jury that's guilty," sputtered the poor, victimized author.

"Of course they are," said the judge, adding with a conspiratorial grin, "but instructions are rather fun, don't you think?" And then, to the jury, "First, fasten your seatbelts. Second, should there be a sudden change in cabin pressure…"

"Those are the wrong instructions," pleaded the anguished one.

"Oh, darn," pouted the judge. "And those are the only ones I know by heart."

"But you've already agreed that they're guilty," said the tormented one. "What about the sentence?"

"Yes, yes, the sentence," said the judge, glee sparkling from his eyeballs. "You must all stand and raise your red pencils…er…and in the case of Susan Corliss, your green one and your yellow one, and your blue one, too. Now then. As you all stand convicted of providing various sorts of help, assistance, advice, and guidance to this miserable wretch of an author in the completion of said manuscript, it is the sentence of this court that your names be carved into the various walls of time so that all who see them will stand in awe of your deeds and applaud them until the wee hours of infinity."

And so it was.